HOW TO BE A GREAT COMMUNICATOR

The Complete System for Communicating Effectively in Business and in Life

Nido R. Qubein

Also by Nido Qubein

Books

ACHIEVING PEAK PERFORMANCE

ATTITUDE

HOW TO BE A GREAT SALES PROFESSIONAL

HOW TO GET ANYTHING YOU WANT

SEVEN CHOICES FOR SUCCESS AND SIGNIFICANCE

STAIRWAY TO SUCCESS

THE TIME IS NOW, THE PERSON IS YOU

UNCOMMON SENSE

CD's

HOW TO COMMUNICATE LIKE A PRO

HOW TO POSITION YOURSELF FOR SUCCESS

HOW TO SUCCEED IN BUSINESS AND IN LIFE

BUILDING A POWERHOUSE BRAND THAT LASTS

EFFECTIVE STRATEGIES FOR MANAGING CLIENT RELATIONS

KEYS FOR BUILDING AND GROWING YOUR BUSINESS

LIFE LESSONS FOR PERSONAL AND PROFESSIONAL GROWTH

NIDO QUBEIN LIVE

POWER MARKETING STRATEGIES FOR YOUR BUSINESS

POWER SECRETS FOR BUILDING YOUR WEALTH MINDSET

THE WISE WAYS OF TRANSFORMATIONAL LEADERS

UNCOMMON SENSE

DVD's

FROM SUCCESS TO SIGNIFICANCE

THE ART OF EFFECTIVE COMMUNICATION

THE POWER OF ONE

Copyright © 2014 by Nido R. Qubein

Library of Congress Cataloging in Publication Data

ISBN 0-9770555-2-3

For quantity purchases of this book contact:

High Point University Press
833 Montlieu Avenue
High Point, NC 27262-3598
(336)841-9201, Facsimile (336)888-6332
www.highpoint.edu

Paperback edition published by John Wiley & Sons, Inc., New York, NY. Available in book stores.

Printed in the United States of America

**To Cristina,
With love.**

ACKNOWLEDGMENTS

—

Occasionally, I forget that I wasn't born in America, that English is my second language, that carving a career in the communication/consulting field is so difficult! By the grace of God, with loving support of family and friends, it has been a mountaintop experience for me. I am so grateful.

And now, as I serve High Point University as its seventh president, I am in awe at the wisdom of our faculty, the dedication of our staff, the loyalty of our alumni, the generosity of our supporters, and the incredibly sparkling spirit of our phenomenal students. I am so blessed and honored to be back at my alma mater and to lead it into an extraordinary future.

When it's all said and done, my life could not have been as meaningful if it weren't for my fellow citizens in my home city (High Point, North Carolina) who accepted me, supported me, and affirmed me with their genuine love. And to the more than 200 leaders who faithfully support our Scholarship Fund, thank you from the bottom of my heart for helping to educate over 600 students. You are kind and generous benefactors.

Contents

Contents

PART ONE

Acquiring the Tools of Communication

Communication: The Requirement of a New Century

On the obstetrics ward at your local hospital, a tiny bundle of humanity squirms its way into the world, draws breath for the first time, and exhales a lusty cry that announces its presence to the universe.

The first overt human act is an exercise in communication.

In time, the squall of the newborn will give way to more complex and more subtle forms of communication. The infant will make eye contact with its parents, will learn to beguile them with a smile, captivate them with its cunning, scold them with a scowl.

But most wondrous of all, it will learn to form those neo-natal wails into words. Later it will learn to put those words onto paper and log them on computer disks. It will learn to send them across miles of distance through fiber-optic cables, through radio signals bounced off orbiting satellites, through feats of technology not yet imagined.

THE GLOBAL TRIBE

These high-tech extensions of the human gift for communication will eventually tie our newborn homo sapiens into a global network that wraps us all in the folds of humanity.

3

In primitive societies, hunters and gatherers stayed in touch mainly through spoken language. Their language was the bond that held them together as a tribe—as a people. Interestingly, most primitive tribes refer to themselves by a word that means "the people," while they refer to other tribes as "those who talk gibberish."

Today, humanity forms a global tribe, and those without good communication skills will find themselves outside the circle of success, among "those who talk gibberish." Those who learn to communicate effectively with people at all levels, of both genders, and from a variety of cultures and backgrounds will be the pace-setters.

Technology will help us to communicate with ever-larger, ever-more-diverse audiences, but technology cannot provide the message. Communication is one function that can't be performed by machines. Communication is a human activity—the foundation of interaction among human beings. Communication has to do with meanings, with understandings, with feelings, with desires, with needs and with ideas. You can't communicate with a computer. Computers only store and process data. They don't have needs, desires, ideas and feelings. Only people have those.

THE BASICS AND THE FINE POINTS

This book is designed to help you develop the communication skills required for the global business environment, and to wield them with power and effect. You'll learn not only the basics, but many of the finer points I've picked up during a long and successful career as a professional speaker, author and adviser to top executives on management and human development.

You'll learn:

♦ The five keys to successful communication.
♦ How to use words and body language effectively.
♦ How to communicate in the work place and in the global mar-

ket with people from different ethnic, cultural and national backgrounds.
- How to speak and write naturally while avoiding sexist language.
- How to communicate with power over the telephone.
- How to get things done at meetings.
- How to communicate effectively from the platform.
- How to put power into your writing.
- How to make effective use of television and the print media to promote your company and enhance your professional image.

PRODUCERS MUST COMMUNICATE

These are no longer "nice-to-have" skills. They are essential to success in the 21st century. To produce and market products and services to billions of people worldwide requires a level of communication undreamed of in previous centuries. When the quality of your product depends upon the collective efforts of dozens, hundreds or thousands of individuals, communication becomes the lifeblood of your enterprise. When the success of your enterprise depends upon the quality of your marketing in China, Turkey, the Netherlands and Nigeria, communication becomes the lifeline of your existence.

THE 21ST CENTURY DIFFERENCE

What makes the 21st century different from previous centuries is the scope of the communication challenge. The challenge is posed at the macro and the micro levels.

The Macro Level: Puddles to Ponds to One Big Ocean

At the macro level, the human race, in previous centuries, existed in puddles of humanity.

In time, some of the puddles sent out feeble streams that inter-connected with other puddles. Nearby puddles enlarged until they joined to form larger puddles, and eventually ponds. But until well into the 20th century, the earth still consisted largely of a European pond, an Asian pond, an African pond and an American pond.

The communication strides of this century have united the ponds and puddles into one great sea, with currents surging from one region to another, but all interacting as a dynamic whole.

The Micro Level: From Patriarchs to Peers

At the micro level, communication has progressed beyond the simple conveying of instructions from patriarch to tribe, from master to slave, from boss to underling. Communication in the modern world is increasingly a matter of interchange among equals.

In the old-style hierarchical, authoritarian setting, communication was relatively simple. The top person tells the underlings to jump, and the underlings need only ask, "How high?"

In a modern organization, communication requires more finesse. The leader is not a transmitter of commands but a creator of motivational environments. The workers are not robots responding to switches and levers, but thinking individuals pouring their ingenuity into the corporate purpose. The corporate ideal is not mechanical stability, but dynamic, innovative, continuous change. The leader who can't communicate can't create the conditions that motivate. The genius who can't communicate is intellectually impotent. The organization that can't communicate can't change, and the corporation that can't change is dead.

COMMUNICATING WITH A DIVERSE WORK FORCE

In the old days, the white male was the undisputed master of the American work force. Although he was a minority in the population as a whole, he was a majority in the work place, and he monopolized top management.

The white male now represents less than half the work force. Women and ethnic minorities constitute the majority. By some estimates, only 8% of newcomers to the work force in the year 2000 will be white males.[1]

This new diversity will force us to learn the subtleties of communicating between the genders with people of different racial, national and cultural backgrounds. Leaders will have to deal not only with different levels of understanding of spoken English, but also with cultural and gender-related differences in non-verbal communication and in the language of motivation.

COMMUNICATION WITH THE MARKET

By some estimates, 85% of your success in business depends on effective communication and interpersonal skills. People must know about your products and services before they will buy them. If your advertising or public-relations messages miss the mark, you've wasted money and you haven't attracted customers or clients. If your salespeople are poor communicators, they won't bring in the revenue. If your customer-service people are inept at communicating, you'll lose business. When customers of one enterprise take their business to a competitor, the villain in the great majority of cases is poor communication.

COMMUNICATION IN THE WORK PLACE

Today's successful company must be alive with communications flowing in all directions, through all levels and divisions.

This requires communication skills on the part of everyone from the CEO to the most junior person on the work floor.

American executives spend 94% of their time in some form of

communication. They must not only communicate with fellow executives, customers, clients and vendors; they must also be able to communicate effectively with the people staffing the offices, running the machines and delivering the services.

James Kouzes and Barry Posner polled more than 7,500 managers nationwide, asking them what qualities they admired in their leaders. Among the most-mentioned qualities were the ability to inspire, the ability to understand the perspectives of others, and the ability to speak with passion. All three qualities express themselves through communication.[2]

Work-place communication is essential to the process of building quality into goods and services. The Federal Quality Institute listed effective communication among the prerequisites for successful quality assurance. Without communication skills, workers can't learn the techniques of statistical process control and other quality measures, much less put them into practice. Quality circles and self-managed teams are ineffectual without good communication skills on the part of their members. Executives, managers and supervisors can't nourish quality-oriented corporate cultures unless they know how to communicate ideas and feelings.

INFORMATION AND RESPONSIBILITY

The switch from authoritarian to participative management has placed a heavy premium on communication skills. Participatory management demands that each individual in the work force take responsibility for corporate success. Uninformed people can't take responsibility. But when you give them information, you confer responsibility upon them.

If your company's earnings are dropping because it has lost control of costs, your employees can't be blamed if you fail to tell them about it. If you explain the situation to them, then you invest them with the responsibility to look for ways to cut costs.

Participative management has ushered in the age of teamwork.

Companies such as Procter & Gamble, Corning, Levi Strauss and many others are investing self-managed teams with responsibilities no 19th century tycoon would have dared delegate to line workers.

Line workers decide how to arrange the machinery in a new plant. They draw up job descriptions, determine staffing levels and take over recruiting. They provide input into budgeting. They decide when to lay off and when to work shorter hours. They maintain their own machinery, and do minor repairs. They advise management when new equipment is needed.

These employees could never handle those responsibilities unless management shared information with them and empowered them to act on the information.

COMMUNICATION IN THE SERVICE ECONOMY

As our economy shifts from manufacturing to service industries, the demand for communication skills is growing. A worker who installs door panels as a car moves down an assembly line needs fewer communication skills than a hotel desk clerk or a software designer.

The Hudson Institute conducted a study for the U.S. Department of Labor and concluded that in the early 21st century, nearly all new jobs created in the United States will be in the service sector. Only 27% will fall in the low-skill category, compared with 40% in 1990. The worker seeking a job in the first decade of the 21st century will have to be able to read at the 11th-grade level. During the '90s, the typical high-school graduate was reading at the 9th-grade level.

So the American work force must sharpen its communication skills from top to bottom. From the boardroom to the work bench, the 21st century is going to require an ability to communicate freely, precisely and clearly.

This kind of communication cannot be accomplished solely by microchips, fiber optics and satellite relays. These artifacts of our technology help to fill the world with information, but information is lifeless without someone to breathe meaning into it. The greatest need is for understanding—for building bridges across the mental and emotional distances that separate human individuals from one another so that we can better live together, work together and get along together.

The leaders of the 21st century must take the initiative in breathing the soul of meaning and understanding into the body of data; of uniting a diverse work force behind a common vision and common goals. They must teach the people they lead to communicate in all directions and at all levels.

Division leaders and department heads must learn to communicate with their peers in other functional areas. Production must communicate with marketing, marketing with product development, product development with sales, sales with shipping; in fact, everybody must communicate with everybody if the company is to tap the full resources of its work teams.

Communication is the essential tool of the salesperson, too. It is fundamental to the art and science of negotiation. It is a vital component of leadership, the principal role of which, according to Tom Peters, is "organizing meanings for people, providing meaning, providing flags to march behind."

It is the tool of corporate intelligence-gathering, an essential activity for those who want to remain abreast of the market and of the competition—in short, of those who want to succeed.

I've invested the last two decades in helping organizations solve problems. This book is a culmination of the lessons I've learned, solutions to the problems I've observed, and a summary of the principles I teach. It will equip the business leaders of the 21st century to practice that most human of talents—communication—and to communicate success to their staffs and work forces. Learning to communicate effectively is an exciting process. We'll begin it in Chapter Two by discussing the five keys to the Kingdom of Communication. Let's roll up our sleeves and get on with it.

CHAPTER

2

The Keys to the Kingdom of Communication

English is my adopted language, and it has served me marvelously. I'd like to repay it by helping others to use it with finesse and success. So I'll share with you the five keys that have opened for me the doors to the Kingdom of Communication.

Some people seem to be born with silver tongues in their mouths. They wield the language the way Joe DiMaggio wielded a bat: purposefully, gracefully and effectively.

But that ability never comes automatically. It has to be learned. The great communicators of history started life just as you and I— with a wordless cry. They had to learn language one word at a time. If you think you don't have the stuff to be an effective communicator, think again. Some of the greatest communicators had to overcome some tough handicaps.

The prophet Moses was, by his own admission, a "meek person, slow of speech." Yet he demanded that the world's mightiest potentate free the conscripted laborers who were making the bricks for Egypt's grandiose building projects. Pharaoh never listened, but 600,000 men, with their wives and families, followed Moses out of Egypt through the parted waters of the Red Sea. And they listened when Moses, face glowing from his encounter with God, descended from Mount Sinai and gave them the law.

You don't have to go up to Mount Sinai to acquire eloquence. All you need to do is to acquire and use the five keys that I'm going to introduce you to.

THE FIRST KEY: DESIRE

My wife Mariana and I have reared four beautiful children—Ramsey, Deena, Cristina and Michael—and we've watched each one slowly acquire the basic tools of language. I can still remember my youngest child, Michael, struggling to tell me he wanted a bottle of fruit juice when he didn't know the words to describe his wishes. It's a frustrating experience for baby and parent.

I experienced the same frustration long after infancy. I came to the United States as a young man with little knowledge of the English language. I had grown up speaking Arabic, a language only remotely connected to English. If I had spoken French, German, Spanish or Italian, I would have had a substantial supply of common words to get me started. But Arabic and English share few words in common, and the beautiful language that has served me so well in my adopted land was then unintelligible to me.

But I had something in common with the baby struggling to communicate. Human infants have an inborn desire to communicate, and that desire enables them to pick up words quickly and to enlarge their vocabularies continuously. I had that desire, too. With the help of countless friends in America, I picked up the language and used it as my instrument for success.

I became a professional speaker, an author and an adviser to corporate leaders across America, and in a dozen other countries. These activities require finely honed communication skills. If I can do it, you can.

In fact, you should find it much easier. I had to invest enormous time and energy in learning the language. If you grew up in America, you already know the language. So if you invest the same amount of time and energy I invested, you should become a virtuoso at communicating.

But to make that investment, you must have the desire to communicate. Moses had it. So did Demosthenes, the Greek statesman whose name has been synonymous with oratory for two thousand years.

Communication Was Greek to Demosthenes

Demosthenes lived during the Golden Age of Greece, when all public disputes were settled by oratory. As a young man, he went before the Assembly in Athens—an unruly legislative body of about 6,000 men—to speak on an important issue. To use a modern English expression, Demosthenes bombed. His voice was weak, his thoughts were muddled and the longer he talked the worse he got. He was hissed and booed off the platform.

Demosthenes vowed it would never happen again.

First, he learned speech writing, and was soon being hired by wealthy men to write their speeches.

Then he went to the shores of the Aegean Sea, where he strengthened his voice by shouting into the wind for hours at a time. To improve his dictation, he practiced speaking with pebbles in his mouth. To overcome his fear, he practiced with a sword hanging over his head. To clarify his presentation, he studied the techniques of the masters.

Years later, Demosthenes stepped before the assembly to warn leaders of the great threat posed by Philip II of Macedonia. He inspired the assembly with his eloquence and laid before it some clearly reasoned ideas for dealing with the Macedonian. When he had finished, the audience rose and shouted in unison: "Let us go and fight Philip."

. . . . And Let Us Go and Fight Hitler

Demosthenes was not alone in overcoming handicaps. Winston Churchill, who is credited with marshalling the English language and sending it to war against Hitler, suffered from a speech impediment as a child. He had to undergo extensive speech therapy during childhood and early manhood.

Franklin Roosevelt had to inspire a demoralized nation from a wheel chair. So effective was his communication that few Americans realized that the man who led them so decisively out of a depression and through a global war could not stand up without braces on his legs.

Helen Keller could neither see, nor hear nor speak. Yet she became an eloquent communicator of the highest order.

Sequoyah was a member of the Cherokee nation who believed that the ability to communicate in writing was the key to empowerment for his people. But though the Cherokee had a rich spoken language, they had no written language. So Sequoyah invented one. In a very short time, the Cherokee became a literate people.

Each of these people had a desire to communicate and exerted the effort to fulfill the desire.

So if you feel timid when confronting other people, tongue-tied when facing an audience, unsure of yourself when putting words on paper, don't give up. Remember Demosthenes, Sequoyah, Keller, Roosevelt and Churchill. Cultivate the desire, and act upon it.

THE SECOND KEY: UNDERSTANDING THE PROCESS

If you want to achieve excellence in communication, you have to cut through the surface and become acquainted with the underlying process. That's what helped Michelangelo achieve greatness as an artist.

Michelangelo wanted to sculpt the human body, but he wasn't sure of what he was sculpting. He knew the body's outward appearance—the general contours of head, torso and limbs. But to render the human body in all its subtleties, he needed to understand the underlying structure.

To obtain this knowledge, he would sneak into a mortuary at

night and carefully cut through the skin of cadavers to examine the muscles, veins and skeletons. It was gruesome work, but it led to some of the greatest art ever to grace the planet. You don't have to go into a morgue to learn the techniques of communicating, but you must learn the underlying structure of the process.

Communicate Through Images

Language is the primary conveyer of thoughts and ideas. It turns abstract concepts into words that symbolize those thoughts. If the mind can immediately translate the sounds and symbols into mental pictures, communication becomes much more vivid and much more meaningful. If I say "I want a desk for my office," my listener has only a vague and general idea of what I want. If I say "I want a brown walnut desk," the listener has a more vivid mental picture. The more skillful you become at conveying images, the more effective your communication will be.

When Paul Revere began the mission that inspired Henry Wadsworth Longfellow's famous poem, he had to row his small boat past a British warship, the *Somerset*. The poet could have written, "Paul Revere rowed past the British warship *Somerset* on his way to Charles Town." But Longfellow visualized the scene: the dark waters, the ship's ominous hulk swinging wide from its moorings, the moon shining through its rigging. He translated his image into words: "A phantom hulk, with each mast and spar across the moon like a prison bar."

We can't all be Longfellows, but we can do as Demosthenes did: study the techniques of the masters and learn from them. We can learn to translate the images and sounds we receive through our eyes and ears into words that will inform and inspire those who hear us.

THE THIRD KEY: MASTER THE BASIC SKILLS

Some people think the first requisite for good communication is an exhaustive vocabulary. Some people think it's impossible to communicate well without first absorbing a heavy dose of grammar, then memorizing a dictionary of English usage.

Words are important. Good grammar is important. And yes, it helps to know which words and expressions are considered standard and which are considered substandard among educated people. But slavish allegiance to the rules of grammar can actually impede communication. People will sometimes go to great lengths to avoid usage that somebody has pronounced "ungrammatical" or "substandard." In the process, they forget the most important rule of communication: Make it clear and understandable.

Winston Churchill showed his contempt for overweening attention to grammar when he was upbraided for ending a sentence with a preposition. He retorted: "This is the sort of English up with which I will not put."

The purpose of communication is to convey ideas, not to show off vocabularies and grammatical expertise. The vocabulary you use in every-day speech has probably served you well. You use the words that you understand. Chances are, they're the words your friends, colleagues and employees understand. If you try to use words beyond the vocabularies of the people you're trying to communicate with, you're not communicating; you're showing off.

Read the Gettysburgh Address, the Sermon on the Mount or Robert Frost's poetry. The communications that endure are written in plain, simple language.

Three Basic Skills

Had I waited until I had amassed a large vocabulary of English words and had a grammarian's knowledge of English, it would have taken me a long time to get started in my career. Fortunately, I didn't have to do that. I recognized the three true basic skills in communication: connecting with an audience, conveying messages people can understand, and checking their responses.

These three basic skills are still fundamental to my work as a communicator.

THE FOURTH KEY: PRACTICE

I first began communicating from the platform while I was an undergraduate student at Mount Olive College in North Carolina. I found that people in the community were interested in what I could tell them about my native country. Those early presentations helped put me through college. Appreciative audiences would pass the hat, and I would take back enough money to keep eating and keep studying.

But I wasn't satisfied with that level of performance or that level of income. I wanted to communicate my way to success, and that meant learning to use the English language fluently and skillfully. This called for practice.

Practice Makes Superb

I remember a story that gave me inspiration. A young musician had listened with awe as a piano virtuoso poured all his love and all his skill into a complex selection of great compositions.

"It must be great to have all the practicing behind you and be able to sit down and play like that," he said.

"Oh," said the master musician, "I still practice eight hours every day."

"Buy why?" asked the astounded young man. "You're already so good!"

"I want to become superb," replied the older man.

To become superb, you have to practice. It isn't enough to know what it takes to connect with people, to influence their behavior, to create a motivational environment for them, to help them to identify with your message. The techniques of communication have to become part of your daily activity, so that they are as natural to you as swimming is to a duck. The more you practice these techniques, the easier you'll find it to connect with people, whether you're dealing with individuals one-on-one or with a group of thousands.

Mental Rehearsal

If you're going to give a speech, imagine yourself on the platform, giving the presentation smoothly, clearly, effectively. Imagine what you will say, how you will say it, and what gestures you'll use. Imagine yourself feeling confident and energized. And—go ahead—imagine a standing ovation at the end.

You can use it just as effectively in rehearsing a presentation to your sales force, to your board of directors, or to the annual meeting of shareholders.

You can practice mental rehearsal for sensitive conversations or sales presentations, too. Imagine what you will say, what the responses will be, and how you will deal with the responses.

If you're planning to write something, get yourself into a relaxed mood and imagine what you would write if you were at your desk at that moment. Many writers get their best ideas while "rehearsing" their writing before falling asleep at night, and even while commuting to work.

This type of practice can be an immense help to you in progressing from the good to the superb.

THE FIFTH KEY: PATIENCE

Nobody becomes a polished, professional communicator on the first try. It takes patience. A few years ago, William White, a journalism and English instructor, edited a book of early writings by Ernest Hemingway.[1] The young Hemingway was a reporter for a Toronto newspaper, and this book was a collection of his articles written between 1920 and 1924.

The writing was good, but it was not superb. It gave a faint foregleam of the masterful storyteller who would emerge in *The Old Man and the Sea,* but it wasn't the Hemingway of literary legend

The Keys to the Kingdom of Communication

What was lacking? Experience. The genius was there all along, but it needed to incubate. The sands of time can abrade or polish. It depends on whether you use your time purposely or let it pass haphazardly.

Hand Rub Your Language

Labor, for the skilled communicator, means constant, careful, loving attention to the craft. Columnist James J. Kilpatrick calls it "hand-rubbing" your communication. Hemingway didn't go from cub reporter to master novelist by jotting down words off the top of his head. He looked at what he wrote, analyzed it, compared it to the best writing he had seen, and looked for ways to improve what he had written. In other words, he engaged in self-evaluation.

The cub reporter didn't transform himself into a successful novelist through one blinding flash of literary insight. So executives shouldn't expect themselves or their employees to become excellent communicators overnight. Your organization's communication skills can be enhanced through a progressive education program that emphasizes continuous improvement. Most people progress from the "good" to the "superb" through hundreds of tiny little improvements from day to day.

That's the way I developed my speaking and writing style. I listened to the best spoken English I could find and tried to model my pronunciation and diction after it. Although I learned English in a small town in North Carolina, I avoided regional accents as much as possible and worked on developing a speech style that would be at home anywhere in America. It has worked for me.

You can use the keys to the Kingdom of Communication in many settings, under a variety of circumstances. Longfellow was a virtuoso as a poet and Hemingway as a novelist, but the field of communication goes far beyond the literary field. You can be a virtuoso at inspiring your work force, at negotiating business deals, at marketing your products and at building a positive corporate image. All these are important communication skills. But always remember: Whatever communication task you undertake, your objective is to connect with people. And that means that your communication must be personal. In the next chapter, we'll explore ways of communicating so that people will identify personally with your message.

CHAPTER

3

All Communication Is Personal

All communication is personal. A mass audience doesn't have a mind. The individuals within that audience have minds. A speech, a broadcast, or a piece of writing, no matter how polished and professional, will have no measurable effect unless it connects with the minds of individuals. It's like a radio signal beamed at a certain frequency. If no radio receiver is tuned to that frequency, the signal vanishes into thin air.

The message-sender must know how to address the personal concerns of the intended message receiver.

THE IMPORTANCE OF DIALOGUE

To establish that personal connection, you have to engage in dialogue. Dialogue, by one dictionary definition, is "an exchange of ideas and opinions."

But dialogue means much more than a swapping of opinions. If I say the United States is a democracy and you say "no, it isn't," and we both drop the subject, nothing has been accomplished. We have swapped opinions, but neither of us has gained much insight into the other's thinking.

But suppose you explain to me that, by your definition, the United States is not a democracy, in which all issues are settled by popular vote, but a republic, in which laws are made by elected representatives. Then I can respond, "I agree that, by your definition, the United States is not a democracy. But to me, a democracy is a government in which people have a right to choose their representatives by popular vote."

Now we have engaged in dialogue. You understand my definition of democracy and I understand yours. Through dialogue, we learn that the similarity between our views is greater than the difference, and we can move on.

Dialogue, by my definition, is *what happens when your reality connects with your audience's reality and together you move toward a new common reality.*

DIALOGUE WITH MASS AUDIENCES

Dialogue doesn't have to take place between two individuals. You can have dialogue with a mass audience too, provided the message you send strikes a personal note with the individuals in the audience.

One of the most stirring examples of dialogue with a mass audience took place at the dedication of the Gettysburgh battlefield on November 19, 1863. The principal address on that occasion was a finely crafted speech delivered by Edward Everett, one of the foremost orators of the day. After he spoke, President Abraham Lincoln delivered a brief secondary speech.

Few people today can recite a single line from Edward Everett's speech at Gettysburgh. Generations of school children have memorized what Lincoln said on that historic occasion.

Lincoln knew his audience. He spoke in simple phrases that nevertheless resonated in the hearts of a nation saddened by civil war. Though the immediate effect on the 15,000 people gathered at the battlefield was unimpressive, the president spoke beyond them to the nation at large and, in fact, to posterity. In moments of national crisis ever since, the American people have drawn courage from his words:

22

. . . . We here highly resolve that these dead shall not have died in vain—that this nation, under God, shall have a new birth of freedom—and that the government of the people, by the people, for the people, shall not perish from the earth."

The words came from the heart of the president and they were aimed straight at the hearts of war-weary Americans. They carried personal meaning for every parent who had lost a son in battle and for every American who despaired for the survival of democracy on the continent. The reality within Abraham Lincoln touched the reality in the hearts of his audience, and together they moved toward a new reality: a stronger, freer America.

Effective communicators know their audiences. They know whom they want to reach and they know how to reach them with messages that touch them personally.

MADISON AVENUE TECHNIQUES

Madison Avenue has become adept at appealing to personal motivations. Watch the next new-car commercial. It will waste very little time detailing the engineering features of the car. People don't buy cubic inches or compression ratios. They buy driving experiences. They buy image. They buy prestige. The ad writers seek to connect with these desires.

"This is not your father's Oldsmobile" was a line aimed at young people who might once have thought of the Olds as a wheel chair for old folks.

AT&T's familiar line, "Reach out and touch someone" is a personal invitation to everyone within reach of a telephone who has loved ones in distant places.

"You got the right one, Baby, uh-huh" tells you nothing about the flavor of Pepsi Cola compared with Coca Cola. But the style and flavor of the commercial clicked with the young audience toward which it was aimed, and soon the youngsters were repeating it and improvising variations of it.

BARRIERS TO DIALOGUE

While the 21st century puts a premium on the art of dialogue, it also raises formidable obstacles to it. Physically and technologically, this is the most connected generation in history.

Psychologically, though, we are a disconnected generation. Bombarded daily with communications of every sort and from every direction, we have had to master the art of tuning out most of the information that comes our way. We have learned instinctively to disregard the "junk mail" and focus on the envelopes that bear personal messages. We have learned to regard the sound from our radios and television sets as background noise until we hear something that concerns us personally. This ability to "tune out" is almost a necessity in this age of the information explosion.

But many of us have tuned in technology and tuned out the human factor. We have become so accustomed to being entertained by our television sets and VCRs, our stereos, boom boxes and video games, that we have almost forgotten what it's like to interact with other humans.

We've learned the art of channel-hopping, flipping remote controls to tune out programming that doesn't interest us. Many people have also developed the art of tuning out the thoughts, the ideas and the emotions of fellow humans. You may notice it when you go into a convenience store and the clerk goes through the mechanics of waiting on you as if it were a transaction between two robots. Salespeople notice it when they call on prospects whose attention spans seem to be about as long as the time it takes to switch channels.

Effective communicators must be able to overcome this tune-out tendency and connect with the personal interests of their audiences. The targets of their messages should say "Aha!" instead of "So what?"

THE FIRST LAW OF EFFECTIVE COMMUNICATION

This brings us to my First Law of Effective Communication: *No worthwhile communication can take place until you gain the complete attention of your audience, and, at the moment you lose that attention, effective communication stops.*

In my speaking career, I developed a simple rule for establishing and sustaining contact with my listeners: The audience is top priority. The first thing I do after I've been introduced to an audience is to get the audience into the act. I find some device that will elicit audience participation, and I proceed with my talk only when I'm sure I have their undivided attention. I look for signs that the audience's attention is straying, and when I see them, I do something to re-establish contact. For example:

- ♦ I ask a question to which the audience can respond.
- ♦ I find a way to become physically involved with the audience and get the audience physically involved with me.
- ♦ I use more humor, anecdotes and audiovisuals.

In Chapter Twenty, I'll share with you more detailed suggestions for getting and keeping your audience's attention.

The principle of involvement doesn't just apply to a speaker addressing an audience. No matter what form of communication you're using, the people you're trying to reach are your audience, and *you have to get them involved.*

YOU HAVE TO GET PERSONAL

Whether you're engaged in advertising, marketing, sales or supervision, you have to get personal. When something becomes personal, it becomes important. You get personal by showing people how they can benefit from listening to your message, or how what you're saying can affect their personal lives.

Lowe's building-supply stores used the personal approach in a series of television commercials showing how ordinary people had made use of Lowe's products in home-improvement projects. A commercial might describe how a family on Elm Street in a small Midwestern town had benefited from using Lowe's supplies. It would conclude by saying that Lowe's provided quality products for building projects "on Elm Street and your street."

Ordinary homeowners who viewed the commercials could identify personally with the people they depicted, and "Elm Street and your street" line reinforced that identification.

When people can make that personal connection between your message and their own lives, good things begin to happen.

When your employees can personally identify with the corporate projects in which they're involved, they will exert themselves to make the projects successful.

One of the secrets behind the spectacular success of the Ford Taurus was the involvement of Ford stakeholders at every level in its design and conception. Team Taurus consulted assembly workers, engineers, sales people, insurance people, suppliers and dealers for ideas about the kind of car they'd like to build, sell and drive. The entire corporate work force could thus take personal pride in the automobile's success.

INVOLVE THE AUDIENCE

Successful companies have found that the secret to effective marketing is to involve their audience—the customer—personally and emotionally. Thus, Prudential doesn't sell insurance policies. It offers its customers the security of owning "a piece of the rock." Kodak generated a lot of business, not by asking people to buy its film but by inviting them to "trust your memories to Kodak." What a powerful way to involve people in your product!

Many people are intimidated by computers and their peripheral accessories. They view them as mysterious, incomprehensible and cantankerous. Therefore, Hewlett-Packard didn't try to sell computers and printers. It advertised, instead, "solutions to unusual problems."

CONNECTING WITH EMPLOYEES

If you're an executive leading a corporate work force, you must always keep the personal interests of your employees in mind. Remember, *people do things for their own reasons; not for yours or mine.* To mobilize their talents and energies behind your corporate goals, you have to show them how their best interests are served by these goals. If they can see personal benefits arising from your corporate goals, then they will become involved in fulfilling them.

But first, you have to establish dialogue. That means listening to others. If you listen to individuals long enough, they'll tell you what their concerns and problems are. Take the time to get to know the people you seek to lead—not just by name, but also by their interests and aspirations. In a friendly way, talk to them about what they did over the week-end, what they plan to do on vacation, what their personal goals are. Then listen. When you listen with open ears and open mind, you'll learn what their interests are. And you'll know how to involve them through personal communication.

CHAPTER 4

The Messenger Speaks Louder Than the Message

If you don't believe the messenger speaks louder than the message, consider these two statements:

(1) *"Haint we got all the fools in town on our side? And ain't that a big enough majority in any town?"*
(2) *"A majority can never replace the man. . . . Just as a hundred fools do not make one wise man, a heroic decision is not likely to come from a hundred cowards."*

The first statement says it with rustic humor. The second statement says it in a loftier tone. But both make the same point: The majority decision isn't always the wisest or the noblest one.

Read them again, this time remembering who uttered them. The first statement is from Mark Twain. The second is from Adolf Hitler. How does your knowledge of the sources alter the message you receive? The odium attached to the name of Adolf Hitler negates any positive element in anything he ever said, and no amount of eloquence will lend it respectability. So if you want to communicate in a positive way, you must cultivate a positive image as a person.

The way people perceive you will depend upon the way you interact with them. We interact with people in one of three basic modes:

- ◆ Superior to inferior.
- ◆ Inferior to superior.
- ◆ Equal to equal.

SUPERIOR TO INFERIOR

The superior-to-inferior relationship can take several forms.

One is the boss-underling relationship. That's the standard relationship between management and employees in the authoritarian work place. We see it in the comic-strip relationship between Dagwood and Mr. Dithers. Charles Dickens described it in his story of Ebenezer Scrooge and Bob Cratchett. That relationship is outdated in the 21st century environment. If you approach employees or colleagues with a superior attitude, you can bet that you'll turn them off. Americans have been thoroughly indoctrinated in the philosophy that all people are created equal. Superior position, superior knowledge, superior expertise and superior experience will win you respect, but only if you display the proper regard for the self-worth of others.

Manipulated Again, Charlie Brown!

The Superior-to-Inferior mode also manifests itself in the methods of the manipulator. The comic strips provide examples of this relationship as well. Garfield the cat is constantly manipulating Odie the dog. In *Peanuts,* Lucy is constantly manipulating Charlie Brown.

Manipulative people are always suspected of having something up their sleeves. Their actions breed attitudes of distrust among the people they work with. The manipulator won't attract a loyal following. Would you trust Lucy to hold the football for you in the big game?

Social Snobbery

Social snobbery is another form of superior-to-inferior relationship. It sometimes comes disguised as *noblesse oblige.* Webster's defines this as "the obligation of honorable, generous and responsible behavior that is concomitant of high rank or birth." But American society is founded on egalitarian principles. The expression "poor but proud" is a defiantly American expression. It captures the idea that wealth and social standing do not confer superiority. If your good deeds are done from the perspective of a superior bestowing favors on inferiors, they will go unappreciated. The recipients will regard you as condescending and patronizing, and will resent you.

Social snobbery often manifests itself on the job as a class distinction between blue-collar and white-collar workers; between degreed and non-degreed employees; between people with advanced degrees and people with bachelor's degrees. It becomes counterproductive when the "superior" refuses to regard the ideas of the "inferior" as worthy of consideration.

The Engineer and the Tool-and-Die Maker

Charles Dygert is a friend of mine who now holds a Ph.D. in vocational education and heads a highly successful consulting business. He began his career as a tool-and-die maker for General Motors. In that blue-collar capacity, he worked from blueprints provided by white-collar engineers.

On one of his first jobs, he discovered a mistake in the blueprint. His fellow tool-and-die makers urged him to follow the blueprint and make the engineer look foolish. They were aware of the blue-collar/white-collar class distinctions and had no love for their "superiors." Charlie was sorely tempted to take their advice, but he decided to correct the error quietly and save the engineer from embarrassment.

Some time later, another engineer approached him with a prototype of a part he wanted to make. He asked Charlie to work with him to design the die to mass-produce the part. As Charlie recalls it, "I gave him six ideas I wouldn't have thought about before." The white-collar engineer showed respect for the blue-collar tool-and-die maker, and it paid off for him.

Charlie tells of another plant in which the blue-collar workers came up with a plan that enabled them to retool a major piece of equipment with only 15 minutes of down time, compared with 12 hours under the procedure set up by plant engineers.

Had the white-collar personnel of that plant practiced social snobbery, the employees would not have gone to them with their idea, and the company would have denied itself tens of thousands of dollars in savings every time it retooled.

Racial or Ethnic Condescension

Another common type of superior-to-inferior attitude is racial or ethnic condescension. We often assume that people with different skin colors, different accents or different-sounding names have inferior communication and comprehension skills.

The story is told of a Euro-American who sat down at a banquet table next to a man who was obviously of Asian descent. Assuming that his companion was Chinese, the Euro-American turned to him during the soup course and inquired, "Likee soupee?"

When the principal speaker was introduced, the Euro-American was surprised to see the man of Asian descent rise and walk to the podium. He proceeded to give a brilliant address in a fluent, middle-American accent. As he sat down, he turned to the Euro-American and inquired, "Likee speechee?"

Remember: The skin color, ethnic background or accent of an individual tells you nothing about the individual's native abilities. Nor does your own skin color, ethnic origin or accent protect you from making a fool of yourself.

INFERIOR TO SUPERIOR

Many gifted people never become all that they could become because they harbor feelings of inferiority. They're afraid to express their own ideas for fear that others know more than they know.

They're reluctant to take the initiative because they feel that others are more qualified.

Truman Took Charge

Harry Truman may have felt that way initially when the weight of the presidency fell on him. He had to step into the shoes of the man many regarded as the greatest president since Abraham Lincoln. He had to assume national leadership at a time when the global political order had been shattered. This ex-farmer, unsuccessful haberdasher, and small-time Missouri politician, who hadn't even gone to college, had to negotiate with the likes of Winston Churchill, Josef Stalin and Charles DeGaulle. He had to give orders to George Marshall, Douglas MacArthur, Dwight Eisenhower, Chester Nimitz and Bull Halsey. He had to deal with the question of nuclear weapons, the existence of which had been unknown to him before taking office. Upon his shoulders fell the weight of rebuilding Europe, stopping communism in Greece, Turkey, Iran, and Korea, and of reconstituting Japan as a friendly democracy. And at home he had to deal with aggressive labor leaders, defiant segregationists who resisted his efforts at dismantling racial barriers, and virulent red-baiters who were willing to sacrifice democratic principles in their zeal to exterminate communism.

Had Truman communicated with Stalin and Churchill as inferior to superiors; had he allowed Douglas MacArthur free rein in the Far East; had he knuckled under to domestic foes with far greater academic and intellectual credentials; had he doubted his own capacity for decision-making; the post-war story would have been far different.

Were all of Truman's decisions the correct ones?

Of course not. Some of them had unfortunate consequences. Some of them are still being hotly debated. But his standing as a leader is unquestioned. In recent elections, presidential candidates of both parties have proudly claimed Harry Truman as a role model.

In whatever field you choose to enter, you will never be any better than you think you are. If you regard yourself as inferior to others, others will regard you as inferior to them. If you confidently assume the role of a leader, others will follow your leadership.

Self Confidence Can Save the Day

Once a group of hikers in the mountains found themselves engulfed by smoke from a forest fire. The fire threatened to encircle them. The smoke obscured all landmarks. They began to stumble in all directions until one of them said confidently, "Follow me."

Linking hands to stay together, they followed the leader. She led them on a straight path through the smoke to safety.

"How did you know the way out?" one of the hikers asked later.

"I didn't," she said, "but I knew we were goners if we didn't get out of there, so I set a course and stuck to it."

The leader had no more knowledge and skill than any of the other hikers. What she had was self-confidence.

The movie classic, "The Wizard of Oz" illustrates the difference a confident attitude makes. You will recall that the "cowardly lion" wanted the Wizard to give him courage. The scarecrow wanted a brain. The tin man wanted a heart, and Dorothy wanted to return to Kansas, where she had lived before a tornado swept her away.

The Wizard had a con man's understanding of human nature. He gave the lion a medal, and suddenly the "cowardly lion" felt brave. He gave the scarecrow a diploma, and at once the scarecrow began acting like a literate person. He gave the tin man a ticking clock, and the tin man took heart. As for Dorothy, he told her that she had always had the power to return to Kansas. All she had to do was to close her eyes and repeat, "There's no place like home." When she did that, her mind conveyed her out of the dream world of Oz and into the real world she had left when the tornado struck.

In social and business relationships, people often have the feeling that they are powerless to remove themselves from an unwanted situation. Abused spouses stay with their abusers because they have allowed themselves to fall into an inferior-to-superior relationship.

Employees tolerate oppressive bosses and sometimes put up with sexual harassment because they see the inferior-to-superior relationship as normal for them. It isn't normal and they aren't helpless. Just as Dorothy had it within her power to return to Kansas, they have it within their power to move out of such situations and into normal relationships.

They don't need a Wizard of Oz. The Wizard performed no magic. All he did was to help the four characters recognize the innate qualities they already possessed. He gave them self-confidence.

You Have the Tools of Greatness

Floyd Wickman, one of the nation's leading sales authors and real-estate educators, languished for years in go-nowhere jobs as a Navy enlisted man, a milkman and a lackadaisical real-estate salesman. Then one day, in a sales workshop, he heard a simple poem that changed his attitude toward himself. The poem, as Wickman recalls it:

Figure it out for yourself, my lad;
You've all that the greatest of men have had:
Two arms, two legs, and a brain to use—
A brain to use if only you choose.[1]

Wickman went on to build a tremendously successful company. One day, in Las Vegas, I gave the keynote address for his Masters Academy and watched first-hand the transformed—and respected executive—in action.

So when you have feelings of inadequacy in the face of others who seem to be more gifted, remember: You have everything it takes to be a leader: two arms, two legs, a brain, a heart, courage, and the ability to go wherever you wish. All you have to do is recognize them.

EQUAL TO EQUAL

The most effective mode of communicating with people is as equal to equal. That doesn't mean that CEOs have to wear coveralls to work and crawl into the grease pits with their line employees.

It does mean that executives, managers and supervisors at all levels must respect the dignity of every person in the organization and communicate with employees on a human-to-human rather than a boss-to-underling basis.

Some companies even refrain from referring to people as "employees." They prefer more egalitarian designations, such as "associates" and "team members." But remember: It doesn't help to change the way you designate positions if you don't show respect for the people in those positions.

Elitist attitudes can be communicated in ways other than words. Do top executives get the choice parking spaces, even when they have no more need for their cars during working hours than does anyone else in the organization? Do they ride up to their executive suites on special elevators, eat in executive dining facilities that are off-limits to ordinary workers, and use gold-plated executive rest rooms that other employees never enter?

Then they are saying to their employees: "We're the elite; you're the unwashed crowd."

In companies such as Medtronic, a Fortune 500 manufacturer of medical electronic devices, even the CEO is required to show a badge before entering a manufacturing facility. This helps to convey to all employees the notion that the CEO is one of them and not some inaccessible and all-powerful entity.

Guides to the Pecking Order

Executives can also establish an aura of superiority through imposing offices guarded by an army of secretaries. These surroundings can be intimidating to those farther down the corporate ladder.

In some organizations, offices are not designed to encourage a flow of communication among corporate people. They are designed, instead, to show where their occupants stand in the pecking order.

A few years ago, Bell Laboratories took a look at its office layout. It discovered that non-supervisory personnel usually shared an office with at least one other person. The office had a glass door so that supervisors could always look in to see what was going on.

Supervisors had private offices. They had glass doors too, but the lower half of the door was frosted, so that you had to stand on tiptoes to see in.

The doors to the offices of department heads had frosted glass from top to bottom. To find out what was going on inside, you had to put your ear to the door and listen.

Executive directors had thick wooden doors. You couldn't see through them and you couldn't hear through them.

Bell Labs redesigned its offices to open up communication channels. The new arrangement had no enclosed offices and no floor-to-ceiling separations of any kind. The work spaces were set off by panels, partitions, furniture and accessories.

Executives, however, shouldn't have to surrender all their privacy. They need some time in which to concentrate on their executive duties, free of distractions. Many executives, while retaining the privacy of their separate offices, set aside blocs of time each day during which they will receive telephone calls and will talk to staffers and employees who feel the need to confer with them.

JOB SKILLS VS PEOPLE SKILLS

The 21st century company can't be run from the ivory tower. You have to get out and touch people. You have to learn how they feel and think and respond. You have to learn about their problems, their joys and their triumphs.

I serve on the board of directors of Southern National Corporation, a regional bank holding company with more than $20 billion in assets. Each of Southern National's corporate executive officers makes it a policy to dedicate one day a month to visiting in the field. They actually go out with their people and meet customers and prospects. They know the people on the front line and the front-line people know them. It has paid great dividends.

This kind of contact gives them great credibility among the people they lead, and this credibility is vital for leadership in the 21st century.

Some people think it's enough to develop the basic career skills. But the career skills required for the 21st century are likely to change often. The long-term skills that will assure success will be in the area of human interaction. They are skills that will serve you within the family unit, within your social circle, within your community and within your business organization. They are the skills that will define you as a total person. That totality constitutes a powerful message.

AVOID RELATIONSHIP PITFALLS

This generation seems particularly hard on personal relationships. The family that stays together from wedding bell to funeral knell is becoming increasingly rare. The number of blended families and one-parent households is on the rise. The individual who can negotiate the 21st-century obstacle course with relationships intact will hold a major psychological advantage in the race for success.

As I've worked with people at all levels of organizations and in a wide variety of settings, I've observed five common causes of failure in personal relationships, whether in business or at home. They are:

- ♦ Preoccupation with self.
- ♦ Hasty assumptions.
- ♦ Negative attitudes.
- ♦ An all-consuming desire to be liked.
- ♦ A disregard for courtesy.

1. PREOCCUPATION WITH SELF

More than 185 years ago, Sir Walter Scott wrote:

> . . . . *The wretch concentered all in self,*
> *Living shall forfeit fair renown,*
> *And doubly dying, shall go down*
> *To the vile dust, from whence he sprung,*
> *Unwept, unhonored, and unsung.*

Nobody likes to deal with the person who is afflicted with the "Big I." Self-centered people monopolize the conversation, and always turn the subject back to *their* opinions, *their* abilities, *their* accomplishments and *their* agenda. They are so concerned about the interests of the "Big I" that they have no time to consider the interests of others.

The word "success" does not contain an "I." The first vowel is the "U," and until we learn to think "you" instead of "I," our batting average in business and in human relations will be close to nothing. The best rule for human interaction is still the one pronounced nearly 2,000 years ago from a hillside in Galilee: "As ye would that men should do to you, do ye also to them likewise." The surest route to success today is to find out what others want, and look for ways to provide it. This applies whether you're trying to maintain a healthy and harmonious home atmosphere, sell goods and services in the global market, or align a work force behind an ambitious vision. Being other-person oriented is a learnable trait. It often comes naturally with maturity.

2. HASTY ASSUMPTIONS

People who jump to conclusions rarely land in the middle of success. We often prejudge people and circumstances by surface appearances without investigating what lies underneath.

A middle-aged man in shabby work clothes walked into the showroom of a Chrysler dealership in Virginia. The salespeople studiously ignored him.

Finally, the owner of the dealership walked over and asked if he could help.

"How much is that car?" asked the man, pointing to the most expensive model Chrysler offered.

The dealer told him.

"I'll take one," said the customer.

"Very good," said the dealer. "And how would you like to finance it?"

"I'll write you a check," said the man.

And so he did. And as he took delivery of his new car, he turned to the dealer once more.

"By the way," he said. "Do you sell dump trucks?"

The dealer proceeded to sell four Dodge dump trucks to this man, who was the owner of a local construction business.

Looks can be deceiving. Success doesn't always wear Brooks Brothers suits and Gucci ties. It can also wear jeans and flannel shirts, coveralls and work gloves, or skirts and blouses.

Misjudging Motives

We often jump to conclusions about the motives of others. It's a human tendency to judge ourselves by our motives but to judge others by their actions. We can always convince ourselves that our motives justify our actions. But when we see someone else committing acts that we disapprove of, we're quick to assign improper motives. Often, too, we assume that we know what people are going to say before they say it. So we jump in and complete their sentences, or we respond to what we *think* they're going to say before they have a chance to say it.

3. NEGATIVE ATTITUDES

You may remember the little guy with the unpronounceable name in the comic strip "Li'l Abner," who went around under a perpetual rain cloud. Wherever he went, things went wrong.

Some people are expert rainmakers. They bring on their bad luck through negative attitudes. They *know* things are going to go wrong, and this faith becomes a self-fulfilling prophecy.

"Cheer up," I once told my friend Bob, who seemed always to be on the losing side of life. "Things could be worse."

"I know," he said. "I once cheered up, and sure enough, things got worse."

"Listen," I said. "If you just have faith that something *good* will happen, something good *will* happen. I want you to believe—really *believe*—that you're going to have a great day tomorrow."

At the end of the next day, I called Bob to ask how his day went.

"Lousy," he said. "Just as I expected."

I had another friend, named Charlie, who was just the opposite. If a load of manure fell on Charlie, he'd say, "Boy, think how this is going to help my strawberry plants!"

No matter what the weather was like, and no matter what his circumstances were, if you asked Charlie how his day was going, he'd say, "Today is the best day of my life."

I once asked him: "Charlie, how is it that every time I see you you're having the best day of your life?"

"Well, Nido," he said, "Yesterday is gone forever and tomorrow is not yet mine. Today is the only day I ever have, so that makes it the best day of my life."

Charlie died a few years ago, but I'm sure that his reward will be an eternity in which each day is the best day of his life.

People loved Charlie. People avoid Bob. They're afraid lightning will strike them or a tree might fall on them while they're around him. And it just might happen.

4. THE DESIRE TO BE LIKED

It's natural to want people to like you. We draw strength and inspiration from our friends. The warm glow of friendship is a great morale booster. But when you try to buy friendship at any price, you cheapen the product. You end up not respecting yourself, and others don't respect you either.

You win respect by setting high standards and living up to them. The Shakespearean counsel is valid in any age:

This above all: to thine own self be true,
And it must follow, as the night the day,
Thou canst be false to any man.

Subordinates often try to curry friendship with the boss by saying what they think the boss wants to hear. When they do this, they serve neither themselves nor the boss. A good executive knows the difference between a friend and a sycophant. Executives need people who are not afraid to bring them the bad news. They respect those who speak up for what they know and believe. If the boss knows you're a "yes person," how much weight will your opinions and advice carry? What you are will speak much louder than what you say.

People who are promoted to positions in which they supervise their former peers often face situations in which duty appears to conflict with friendship. The answer to that dilemma was provided by the Greek philosopher Sophocles 2,400 years ago: "I have nothing but contempt for the kind of governor who is afraid, for whatever reason, to follow the course that he knows is best for the state; and as for the man who sets private friendship above the public welfare—I have no use for him either."

What's true in the realm of public office is also true in the business setting. Stay true to your principles. Your true friends will respect you for it. The friendships you'll lose because of it are not worth having in the first place.

5. DISREGARD FOR COURTESY

Some people go to the opposite extreme. They interrupt people at will, and they say what's on their minds without regard for the other person's feelings. They think the world should run on their schedule, so they show up for appointments when it's convenient, and if they keep others waiting, that's tough. Concessions are for weaklings and diplomacy is useful only as a manipulative tool.

Such people may be able to bulldoze their way to success for a while. But when they encounter reverses and they find themselves in need of supporters, they'll find more gloaters than sympathizers.

Courtesy is the oil that lubricates the machinery of commerce. It smooths the path to success in sales, in management and in personal relationships. For courtesy usually is reciprocated. When you open the door for your companion, your companion will usually open the next door for you. If you listen without interruption to the person who is addressing you, that person usually will listen without interruption to you.

If courtesy isn't reciprocated, don't resort to rudeness in return. The most devastating response to a discourteous act is an act of calm, deliberate courtesy.

You Are a Powerful Medium

You can't find a more powerful medium of communication than yourself—your character, your personality and your principles.

If you want to send a powerful, positive message to the people with whom you work, follow these principles:

(1) *You manage the process, but you LEAD people.*

An organization runs smoothly when its people function smoothly. Dealing with problems in engineering, production, marketing and sales without dealing with the human element is like dealing with a flat tire without dealing with air. The finest steel-belted radial is worthless without the air that holds it up. The finest engineering, manufacturing, marketing, sales and servicing systems are worthless without the people who keep them functioning.

In an interview with Harvard Business Review, Robert Haas, chairman of the board of Levi Strauss, called production-management "the hard stuff" and people management "the soft stuff."

Under the old philosophy at Levi Strauss, he said, "The soft stuff was the company's commitment to our work force. And the hard stuff was what really mattered: getting pants out the door. What we've learned is that the soft stuff and the hard stuff are becoming increasingly intertwined."

So pay careful attention to the human side of your business.

(2) *Inspire people, don't just drive them.*

We can inspire people by showing them how to be their very best. Ed Temple, the Tennessee State track coach who worked with some of America's top women's track stars, liked to say, "A mule you drive, but with a race horse, you use finesse."[2] Treat your people like Thoroughbreds instead of like mules. They'll get the message and respond.

(3) *Be easy to respect and look up to.*

You don't gain respect by sitting in an ivory tower and looking down on the work floor. Be accessible to employees and let them see your human side.

Employees are turned off by executives who pretend to be infallible. Observe high standards of personal conduct, but let your employees know that you're human. Talk to them about your bad decisions as well as your good ones. When you blow it, grin and admit it. Your employees will respect you for it.

(4) *Be easy to like and get along with.*

Employees like leaders who are human—who make mistakes and acknowledge them. It's all right to let them see your vulnerability. If you made a bad decision, talk about it with the people you lead. Let it be a lesson for them as well as for you.

Don't feel that you have to know everything. Acknowledge that the people you lead may know much more than you do about certain things.

(5) *Help people to like themselves.*

Robert W. Reasoner, a California school superintendent, who headed a statewide task force on self-esteem, identified five basic attitudes that foster self-esteem. They are:

- ◆ A sense of security.
- ◆ A sense of identity.
- ◆ A sense of belonging.
- ◆ A sense of purpose.
- ◆ A sense of personal competence.

Secure people are comfortable with who they are and with what others think about them. They know their roles in the organization and are confident that they can fill them.

People with a *sense of identity* know how they fit into the work place and how the work place fits into their lives. To them, work takes its place among family, friends and community as an important and fulfilling component of their lives.

When employees have a *sense of belonging,* they identify with the company's vision and goals, because these things have personal meaning for them. They personally share in the success and the prestige of the company.

Employees obtain a *sense of purpose* from knowing the company's goals and knowing how their efforts contribute toward those goals. Management needs to take employees into its confidence and give them a role in planning and goal-setting. You can give employees a *sense of personal competence* by educating them for their jobs and giving them the freedom to succeed or fail on their own.

(6) *Help people to believe that what they're doing is important.*

My friend Stew Leonard, the grocery-store wizard from Connecticut, once told me that he refused to use job titles that he perceives as demeaning. Once he noticed a job listed as "popcorn maker." He immediately ordered a more dignified title.

"How would you feel if someone asked you what you did for a living and you had to answer, 'I'm a popcorn maker'?" he asked me.

Are there any demeaning titles in your organization?

Medtronic, Inc., has a heartwarming way of dramatizing the importance of what its employees do. Each year at Christmas time, the company holds a party for employees. Guests of honor are people whose lives have been prolonged by Medtronic cardio-pulmonary devices.

Can you think of ways of dramatizing to your employees the importance of what they do?

(7) *Be responsive to people. Listen to people. Read people. Respond; don't react.*

Leaders should be accessible to the people they lead. Let your staff and associates know they can come to you with problems, concerns, ideas, suggestions or complaints. If they bring you usable ideas, adopt the ideas and give the employees credit.

Welcome bad news as well as the good. What you don't know can hurt you. Don't ignore complaints. Listen to them. Find out what you can do to rectify matters, let the employees know what you plan to do—and do it.

If you put these principles into practice, you will be constantly sending out a powerful and positive message: Yourself.

The Messenger Speaks Louder Than the Message

Humans have a variety of ways to send messages. We "speak" with our eyes, our facial expressions, our posture, our clothes, our grooming, our lifestyles, and many other aspects of our persons. But the most familiar and most explicit form of communication is with words. In the next chapter, we'll explore ways to use words for maximum impact.

Choosing Your Words

You learned in kindergarten that "Sticks and stones may break my bones, but words can never harm me."

Don't believe everything you learned in kindergarten. In the world of politics and statecraft, choosing the wrong words can lose elections, precipitate wars, and destroy cities. In the world of business they can alienate clients, drive away customers and land you in law suits.

When you write a business letter, draft a proposal, dictate a report, address your employees, speak to a community organization or negotiate a business deal, words can be powerful tools of success or instruments of self-destruction.

A QUARANTINE TO AVERT WAR

Ask the Russians. In 1962, President John F. Kennedy was presented with convincing evidence that the Soviet Union was setting up bases in Cuba for nuclear-tipped missiles that could threaten American cities. Soviet ships might soon arrive bearing missiles and nuclear warheads. The president weighed his options. The United States Navy could *blockade* the Cuban coast, but a blockade would be an act of war. A war between the Soviet Union and the United States would surely escalate into a nuclear conflict.

Kennedy declared that no nuclear weapons would be allowed into Cuba. But he didn't call it a blockade. He called it a *quarantine.* That face-saving word allowed the Soviet leader, Nikita Khrushchev, to back down without acquiescing to an act of war. It's possible that one word avoided a nuclear holocaust.

THE VALUE OF WORDS

In the world of business, words convey instructions and inspiration to the people who produce goods and services. They are the medium through which merchandise is marketed and sold. They provide directions for those who ship and deliver. And they convey directions for assembling and using the products.

The quality of a company's communications can have a significant effect on the image it projects to its customers and clients. Letters that have a professional ring inspire confidence in your organization. And precision in the use of language can save you money when you're making proposals, entering agreements or quoting specifications.

The way you use words influences the way people size you up as a business person. A person who uses language fluently and grammatically is likely to exert much more influence than one who uses it ineptly by mispronouncing and misusing words and by using poor grammar.

That doesn't mean that your grammar must be impeccable and that you must know—and use—every word in the dictionary. It simply means that you stand a much better chance of succeeding in the business world if your speaking and your writing identify you as an educated person. In the world of business, as in the worlds of politics and statecraft, the ability to communicate clearly, precisely and eloquently in spoken and written language is a prime asset. The English language is made up of about 800,000 words. Fortunately, you don't need to know all of them to communicate effectively. We use only about 800 words in our daily conversation. Words must be used with care, however, because their meanings are often slippery. Those 800 everyday words that we use can have about 14,000 different meanings.

SLUGGING AWAY

To illustrate:

You drink a slug of orange juice in the morning before leaving for work. You read in your morning paper that doctors removed a .22-caliber slug from the shoulder of a robbery victim. As you step outside your front door to pick up your newspaper, you avoid a slimy slug crawling across your lawn. In the cafeteria at your office building, you try to put a quarter into the coffee vending machine, but it won't accept your money. Somebody has dropped a slug into the slot and jammed it. It makes you so mad you want to slug the person who did it.

In that simple story, the word slug had five different meanings. Other common words have many more. Webster's Third New International Dictionary lists more than 40 meanings for the word *run* and more than 30 for *ring*.

REGIONAL VARIATIONS

Meanings of common words may vary from region to region. In most places, if you invite people to dinner, you expect them to arrive some time after six. But in some places, you'd better expect them around noon. Most Americans refer to the midday meal as lunch and the evening meal as "dinner." But in some areas, people have their "dinner" in the middle of the day and eat "supper" before going to bed.

A mess is an untidy situation unless you're in the military service, in which case it refers to a meal. In the rural South, a "mess" refers to the quantity of a commodity required for a family meal.

If you're in Georgia and you're told to "mash the button" for the third floor, don't try to crush the elevator button. You're simply being requested to press it. In South Carolina, a young man might say to his girlfriend's father, "Can I carry your daughter to the picture show?" The father, if he's also from South Carolina, won't throw the young man out. He'll understand him to mean, "May I escort your daughter to the movie?"

So before you speak and before you listen, look around to see where you are.

STANDARD ENGLISH IS ALWAYS AT HOME

Despite variations from one locale to another, from one social group to another, and from one ethnic group to another, North Americans generally employ a mutually comprehensible dialect called Standard American English. England, Australia and New Zealand also have their standard versions of the mother tongue.

For Americans, Standard English is the language of the national television newscast, which communicates to almost every level of society. Wherever you live, if you learn to use the standard dialect of your language, it will serve you in almost every business and social setting you're likely to encounter.

THE MULTI-LINGUAL HERITAGE OF ENGLISH

The English language in all its dialects has been enriched by borrowed words from many different languages, including Latin, German, Greek, Celtic, French, Spanish, Italian, Danish, Yiddish, Arabic, Chinese, and Japanese. It also has drawn upon American Indian and African tribal languages. For example, a farmer may raise *swine* (Anglo-Saxon). When he kills and butchers one of the *hogs* (Celtic) he puts *pork* (French) on the table, perhaps accompanied by *succotash* (Algonquian).

52

The foundation of modern English is the Germanic Anglo-Saxon language. In the year 1066, the French-speaking Normans conquered England, and for the next couple of centuries the French language blended with the Anglo-Saxon, giving rise to modern English. French, in turn, is an offspring of Latin, the language of the Roman Empire.

Today, most of the words in the English dictionary are derived from Latin. But most of the words we use in everyday speech are from Anglo-Saxon.

SHORT AND STRONG VS. SCHOLARLY AND LOFTY

As a general rule, Anglo-Saxon words are shorter and more energetic than Latin words. Latin words often are considered more elegant and more scholarly, perhaps because they were the words used by the French-speaking nobility after the Norman conquest. Sometimes Anglo-Saxon words are considered crude while their Latin synonyms are considered usable in polite company. Thus "Huxley's Whores" in the novel, **Battle Cry** became "Huxley's Harlots" in the movie, which was made before Hollywood adopted the policy of "anything goes." Many newspapers refused to advertise Larry King's "The Best Little Whorehouse in Texas," although they probably would not have objected to "The Best Little House of Prostitution in Texas." **Whore** is Anglo-Saxon and **prostitution** and **harlot** are Latin.

We **sweat** in Anglo-Saxon and **perspire** in Latin. We **think** in Anglo-Saxon and **cogitate** in Latin. We **talk** in Anglo-Saxon and **converse** in Latin. We **work with our hands** in Anglo-Saxon and **perform manual labor** in Latin. Anglo-Saxon **food** is Latin **victuals.** Anglo-Saxon **cooking** is Latin **cuisine.** Anglo-Saxon **chicken** is Latin **poultry.** You **teach** in Anglo-Saxon; you **educate** in Latin.

You'll notice that most of the Anglo-Saxon words have one syllable while most of the Latin words have more than one.

Winston Churchill maintained that "Short words are best, and the old words, when short, are best of all." Churchill's language surged with strong Anglo-Saxon terms.

But you don't need to become an expert on Latin and Old English to choose the right words. Use the simplest, most familiar words in your vocabulary that express the thought you want to express the way you want to express it. Pretend that you're writing to Winnie the Pooh, who said, "I am a bear of very little brain, and long words bother me."

In his Gettysburgh Address, Lincoln used four Anglo-Saxon words for every word of Latin origin, but the Latin words gave the speech dignity and loftiness. The phrase, "Conceived in liberty and dedicated to the proposition that all men are created equal," contains eight Anglo-Saxon words and only six of Latin origin. But the Anglo-Saxon words are mainly connectors. The Latin words—"conceived," "liberty," "dedicated," "proposition," "created" and "equal"—convey the bulk of the meaning and provide the dominant flavor. However, the expression "of the people, by the people, for the people" is pure Anglo-Saxon.

FAD WORDS THAT STICK AROUND

Some people ignore Churchill's advice and shun plain old words in favor of fancy new words. President Warren Harding promised to return the country to "normalcy" instead of getting us back to normal. During the Eisenhower administration, people stopped completing things and started finalizing them. During the Kennedy administration, people started having "judgments" instead of opinions.

John Dean, the Nixon staffer who blew the whistle on Watergate, later recalled that during his congressional testimony he was under a great deal of tension because he needed to use the bathroom. Dean would have achieved relief a lot quicker had he avoided the lengthy expressions "at this point in time" and "at that point in time" and said simply "now" and "then."

These long, pretentious expressions have become the favorite retreat of the bureaucrat, who follows the maxim: "When in doubt, obfuscate." (You could say "When in doubt, make it hard to understand," but "obfuscate" sounds more bureaucratic.) But, in the office, on the work floor and in daily conversation, you'll be understood better and you'll make a better impression if you choose the most commonly understood words and say them in the most direct way.

WORDS WITH SEMANTIC BAGGAGE

Some words to be particularly careful with are those that carry meanings that go beyond their dictionary definitions. They come with what we call "semantic baggage."

Let us take the words "denomination," "sect" and "cult." All three have similar literal meanings. Essentially, each refers to a group of people with common religious beliefs. But most people think of a **denomination** as one of the "mainline," "respectable" religious bodies: Roman Catholics, Baptists, Methodists, Presbyterians, Episcopalians and Lutherans, for example, within the realm of Christendom. A **sect** is somewhat less respectable. It usually refers to a less popular group whose teachings are not entirely acceptable to the majority. But when we hear the word **cult,** we think of Satanic worship, the Jonestown tragedy, or David Koresh's ill-fated Davidian Branch of Waco, Texas. Each word carries "semantic baggage."

The word "capitalism" has a perfectly respectable pedigree, but for much of the 20th century it was used in a derogatory sense by adherents of communism. It therefore acquired semantic baggage. Those who practiced capitalism preferred to refer to it as "private enterprise" or the "free-enterprise system."

"Propaganda" is a neutral term roughly equivalent to "advertising" in most parts of the world, but in the United States "propaganda" is considered to be a shady distortion of the truth.

People often reveal their political and social views by the words they use. "Red China" is a generally pejorative term for the country that calls itself the People's Republic of China. If you call it by its official name, people may think you're a bit leftist in your leanings. "Mainland China" is a more neutral term, and one preferred by most people who do business with the Chinese. It's one way of avoiding the question of whether the communist government on the mainland or the Nationalist government on Taiwan is the legitimate ruler of China.

SLANG ISN'T ALWAYS 'WITH IT'

Some people like to use slang expressions or "street talk" to show that they're up-to-date. In spoken English, slang expressions can carry impact when used on the right audience by the right person, but there are pitfalls. People who are unaccustomed to using slang may find that some expressions have subtle meanings of which they're unaware. The results can be unintended insults, which can alienate whole categories of people. If slang isn't a natural form of expression for you, don't use it. If you do, it may be as noticeable to the audience as will the accents of the Russian native practicing newly learned English.

When writing, remember that slang expressions have short lives. If you don't believe it, go to the microfilms and read some newspaper issues from the '30s and '40s. The slang expressions that were current then sound quaint and dated today. The average life span of a slang expression is about four years—the length of a high-school career.

DON'T BE VAGUE, MORE OR LESS

When you speak or when you write, be as specific and as definite as you can. Words such as *several, many, few, various, recently,* and *in the near future* are vague and they rob your language of power.

"We will complete the project by August 1," is a much more

56

powerful sentence than "We expect to complete the project in the near future."

The expression *etc.* for *et cetera* or *and so forth* saps your language of power. How would the British people have responded had Churchill told them, "I have nothing to offer but blood, toil, tears etc."?

Watch out for words that seem to have indefinite meanings but actually mean specific quantities. A *score* is 20. A *myriad* can mean "a large number," but it also refers to a specific number: 10,000. And when using large numbers be aware of the differences between British and American ways of counting. In the United States, a *billion* means one thousand million (1 followed by nine zeroes). In Great Britain, it means one million million (1 followed by 12 zeroes). The American billion is called a *milliard* in Britain. The British billion is called a *trillion* in the United States.

Beware also of words that have deceptive meanings. *Presently* can mean *currently,* or it can mean *soon.* To make sure you're understood accurately, use the unambiguous term. A *suggestive* remark is not a simple suggestion; it is a remark tinged with impropriety. *Ingenious* means clever. *Ingenuous* means candid. To *forbear* is to refrain from, or desist. A *forebear* is an ancestor. A *foregone* conclusion is a conclusion known in advance. *Forgone* interest is interest that has been forgiven.

IT'S BEST NOT TO LITERALLY DIE

Many people use "literally" as an intensifier to add emphasis to a statement. But to take a word "literally" means to take it at its dictionary meaning. When you say "I literally died from embarrassment," you're saying that you actually died, although few people have literally died and come back to tell about it.

Other commonly misused words:

Infer means to draw a conclusion based on certain information. To *imply* means to indicate indirectly. Remember: The message sender *implies;* the message receiver *infers.*

57

Comprise means to *include.* When you see the expression "comprised of," you know that the word is being used incorrectly. The United States *comprises* 50 states and the District of Columbia. You can also say that the United States is *composed of* 50 states and the District of Columbia.

Unique doesn't mean "unusual" or even "very unusual." It means one of a kind. Something is either unique or it isn't. A thing cannot be "most unique" or "somewhat unique." Nor can one thing be more unique than another. If it's "almost unique," just say it's *rare* or *unusual.*

POWER ROBBERS

Writers and speakers often rob their language of power by using weasel words or qualifying expressions. Suppose Jefferson had written: "We hold these truths to be more or less self-evident." Imagine Lincoln referring to "the government of the people, by the people, for the people, in a manner of speaking." Or Admiral Perry exhorting, "Don't give up the ship, if you can help it."

State your convictions in strong, unequivocal words. That doesn't mean that you must always be blunt and undiplomatic. It simply means that you express your ideas clearly and confidently.

STABILITY AMID CHANGE

In the era of rapid change, language will change too. The tide of immigrants from other cultures, speaking other languages, inevitably will add new words to the English vocabulary. The advance of technology will necessitate the coinage of new words. At the end of the 19th century, words such as *antibiotics, television, microwave* and *computer* were unknown. If a New York businessperson in 1955 had asked a client in San Francisco to "fax me that information," the client would not have understood. In 1975, only a few initiates would have understood such terms as **microchip, RAM, megabyte, software, hard drive** and **baud rate.** In 1985, you would have drawn a blank stare if you had mentioned a CD ROM.

But if communication is to remain precise, meanings of common words need to remain stable. So Churchill's preference for "short words" and "old words" makes sense. When an old, short word expresses an idea accurately and adequately, use it. Turn to neologisms—new words—only when the old ones are inadequate to the task.

If you use words that are familiar to you and to your audience, the chances of misunderstanding are minimized. And in business, as well as in statecraft, misunderstandings can be costly. If you're offered a chance at a leveraged buyout of a British company for a billion dollars, count the zeroes before you sign the papers.

Words are a uniquely human form of communication, but they by no means represent the full range of human expression. In fact, some of our most important communication is wordless. In Chapter Six, we will look at the many fascinating ways we send messages without words.

CHAPTER 6

Communicating Without Words

Most of the communicating you do is wordless. The moment you enter the presence of another person you start communicating. Your physique, your clothing, jewelry, voice qualities, facial expressions, posture and many other factors pass along important information. They give information or clues as to social, marital and financial status, your sex, and personal taste.

When you speak, your voice speaks in ways that go beyond words. Your accent may give away your national or regional origin. Your tone of voice will tell people whether you feel elated or sad, excited or bored.

Through verbal communication, people learn about your thoughts and ideas. Through non-verbal communication, they learn about your feelings.

About 93% of your communication is non-verbal. Much of it is unconscious, but you can bring a great deal of your wordless communication under conscious control.

Your media for non-verbal communication fall into four broad categories:

♦ Voice quality.
♦ Body language.
♦ Facial expressions.
♦ Clothing and grooming.

VOICE QUALITY

Often, how we say things conveys more meaning that what we say. In fact, voice quality is said to convey about 38% of your meaning.

Once G. K. Chesterton, the British writer and critic, went into a fish market and tried an experiment. To the woman waiting on him, he said in a low, endearing voice, "You are a noun, a verb and a preposition."

The woman blushed, apparently flattered that such a cultured individual had observed such qualities in her.

After buying the fish, Chesterton said in a higher voice, "You are an adjective, an adverb and a preposition."

The woman slapped him with a flounder.[1]

Taken literally, Chesterton's words were meaningless. To call someone an adjective—whatever that means—is certainly no more insulting than to call one a noun. But the tone of voice conveyed a meaning that the woman understood instinctively, and her response was instinctive.

In your daily interactions, it's important to pay attention to voice qualities. You supervise, teach, inspire, encourage, sell, praise and reprimand with your voice, and much of your meaning is conveyed through media other than words.

When George Bush ran for president in 1988, he hired a voice coach to help him lower his voice an octave. Why? Because the candidate's high-pitched voice had helped saddle him with the "wimp" image, even though Bush had proved his valor as a Navy combat pilot during World War II.

Fairly or unfairly, we impute strength and confidence to the person who speaks with a low-pitched, well-modulated voice. When the voice rises to a high pitch, we sense excitement, panic, and lack of control. That doesn't mean that we should all go around cultivating baritone voices. It simply means that each of us should use the lower end of the voice range when we want to communicate calmness, confidence and competence.

We convey feelings, moods and attitudes through a variety of voice qualities, which are sometimes called paralanguage. Among these qualities are volume, pace, intonation, stress and juncture.

Volume and Pace

Volume and pace should be used in a careful, controlled way. These qualities can work in unison to achieve powerful effects, especially when speaking from the public platform. You can let your voice rise to a crescendo, the pace and volume quickening until you reach a peak of excitement. Or you can drop to a dramatic whisper.

Volume should always be great enough that you can be heard by everyone you're trying to reach with your voice. When addressing a group through a microphone, that generally presents no problem for you. When speaking without a microphone, keep checking the people farthest from you for signs that they're straining to hear, or indications that their attention is straying.

Pace should be adapted to the message. Some simple but telling points can be made effectively in rapid-fire sequence. Others can be made by slowly drawing out the words, or by long pauses to let the points sink in.

We can imagine that Abraham Lincoln spoke in calm, measured tones as he opened the Gettysburgh Address with the words, "Fourscore and seven years ago, our forefathers brought forth . . . ." He probably spoke a little faster as he concluded with ". . . . the government of the people, by the people, for the people shall not perish from the earth."

We can imagine Patrick Henry's volume and pace increasing as he concluded his famous oration to the Virginia Convention in Richmond:

> *What is it that the gentlemen wish? What would they have? Is life so dear or peace so sweet as to be purchased at the price of chains and slavery?*

*Forbid it, Almighty God. I know not what course others
may take, but as for me, give me liberty or give me death!*

You may never be called upon to dedicate a battlefield or to exhort your comrades to take up arms. But business leaders are constantly called upon to instruct, explain, advise, exhort and inspire,
and the same principles apply. You will use a different pace when explaining your profit-sharing plan to line workers from the one you
use when congratulating your sales staff on setting a new record.
You'll probably use a slow, calm delivery when explaining the details
of an acquisition proposal to your legal staff. You'll be more animated when breaking the news of a promotion to a rising executive.
Criticism and reprimands are usually more effective when delivered
in a calm, measured voice.

Intonation

Intonation refers to the voice pitch. We usually speak in a range
of pitches from low to high. Chesterton used low intonation when he
called the woman in the fish market a "noun, a verb and a preposition." He used high intonation when he called her an "adjective an
adverb and a conjunction." His intonation provided the meaning that
was lacking in his words.

The range between high and low intonations varies from individual to individual, and from one linguistic population to another. The
English generally have a greater range than do Americans.

Intonation can enliven your conversation, but don't go to extremes. Linguist Katharine LeMee tells of the Englishman and American who addressed the same Egyptian audience. The Englishman's
words were more complimentary than those of the American, but the
Egyptians responded more positively to the American. The reason
lay in the intonations. The Englishman's clipped Oxford accent was
taken as somewhat aristocratic and disdainful, as if he were talking
down to the Egyptians. The American's flatter, less modulated intonation came across as more sincere and democratic.[2]

Stress

Stress is another important element of paralanguage. The way you emphasize words can change the meaning of your sentences.

Notice how stress changes the meaning of this sentence:

- ◆ *Mary* only takes classes in accounting. (Mary takes classes only in accounting, but others may take classes in other subjects.)
- ◆ Mary *only* takes classes in accounting. (Mary takes classes in accounting, but nobody else does.)
- ◆ Mary only *takes* classes in accounting. (Mary doesn't *teach* the classes; she just *takes* them.)
- ◆ Mary only takes *classes* in accounting. (Mary isn't an accountant; she's just studying accounting.)
- ◆ Mary only takes classes in *accounting.* (Mary takes classes in accounting, but in no other subjects.)

As you speak, be conscious of the effects of sense stress on the meaning you're trying to convey. Use stress to help your listener understand the sense in which you use words and to show which words you consider to be important.

Juncture

Juncture refers to the way vowels and consonants are joined in the stream of speech. If you listen to someone speaking in a foreign language, it sounds like a continuous flow of syllables. That's because you haven't learned to recognize the signs that tell you where one word stops and another begins.

Speakers of other languages have the same problem comprehending English. As I've spoken on different continents, I've formed a great admiration for the translators who have had the task of rendering my speech into other languages. Once I was translated simultaneously into seven different languages. Either my juncture was good or my translators were superb. The audiences laughed at the appropriate points and applauded at the appropriate points.

Some combinations, though, will throw even native speakers of English. An elementary-school teacher once told her geography class, "Malaya is not as big as Siam." One of her pupils went home and told her parents, "Malaya is not as big as my teacher."

So pay close attention to the way you join the sounds of different words, especially if you're dealing with people who are new to the English language.

Juncture will vary from one speaking population to another. To a native of New Jersey, the last syllable in Trenton is pronounced just like the "ton" in "ten-ton truck." A Carolinian would de-emphasize the final syllable and call it TRENT'N. When Britons say "military," they barely pronounce the "a." They join the "t" and the "r" as if they were one consonant. When Americans say it, the "tar" is pronounced clearly, with almost as much stress as is put on the first syllable. To the Briton, it's MIL-i-t'ry. To the American, it's MIL-i-tar-y.

To take a more extreme example, note the different meanings that emerge when you vary the juncture on the syllables in *notable:*

>The **notable** surgeon was **not able** to perform the operation because he had **no table.**

Inattention to juncture can make your speech indistinct or hard to understand. If you tell a carpenter to build a greenhouse, make sure that you don't end up with a green house. The difference in appearance and cost can be substantial. If you ask your secretary to get you the night rate and have it on your desk the next morning, be sure it doesn't sound like "nitrate." Otherwise, you may find a sack of fertilizer in your "in" basket.

Laughing, Crying, Yawning, Sighing

Other aspects of paralanguage convey important signals during speech. Laughter, crying and sighing are among the more obvious signals. The meaning of the sentence, "I fell down the stairs," changes dramatically when spoken with a laugh and when spoken through tears. "Tell me how you plan to market that new product you're proposing," sounds much more upbeat when preceded by a sharp whistle than when accompanied by a yawn. "Janet, you misspelled Iacocca again," sounds much less threatening when said with a chuckle than when said with a sigh.

Every language has its little clicks, whistles and throat noises that don't show up in dictionaries, but which serve useful functions in conversation. When you're talking on the telephone and hear nothing but silence on the other end, you may wonder whether the connection has been broken or the other party isn't listening. An occasional "Hmmm," "unh," and "yeah," will assure you that you have the other's attention.

BODY LANGUAGE

While your tongue is conveying oral communication, your body is talking, too.

As soon as you stop to talk to someone, you make a statement. How close do you stand to the person you're talking to?

Each of us walks around in a bubble of space that expands or contracts according to the person with whom we're interacting.

The poet W. H. Auden wrote:

> *Some 30 inches from my nose,*
> *The frontier of my person goes.*

We can assume that Auden spoke to people from a distance of at least 30 inches. Some people move in closer. Some maintain greater distances. Individuals from some Somali tribes in East Africa have personal bubbles 7 feet in diameter.

We usually stand closer to friends and loved ones than we do to strangers. So when you're speaking to people on the job or in business relationships, be conscious of their personal bubbles of space. If you notice them backing away from you, don't try to move in. They're establishing a distance that's comfortable for them.

Some cultures tend toward smaller bubbles and some toward larger ones. The animated Italian will move in closer than will the reserved Londoner. Hispanic Texans will move in closer than Nordic Minnesotans. If you move in a rather large bubble and you supervise or manage people who recognize smaller bubbles, you might consider using a larger desk to keep people from crowding you.

Your Posture Sends a Message

After you've established a comfortable distance, notice your posture. Posture can tell your conversational partner a great deal about your attitude. An alert, erect posture signifies interest and involvement. A slouching posture says, "I'm not really interested in exchanging ideas with you." A stiff, rigid posture says, "I don't feel fully comfortable in your presence."

When you stand face to face with an individual, your feet pointed straight toward the feet of the other person, you're signaling to others that this is a private conversation. When you stand so that your bodies form two sides of a triangle, you're inviting others to join you.

Voiceless Signals

A number of voiceless signals can be used to indicate that a conversation is over. If you're seated, you can end the discussion simply by rising. If you're in a crowded room talking to an individual and you're ready to move on to another conversation partner, just direct your eyes away from the person you're talking to.

Talking With Your Hands

Most people talk naturally with their hands. As you speak, your hand movements accompany your words, punctuating them, illuminating them, driving them home. Hand gestures are particularly important when speaking to groups, because they help keep the listeners' attention focused on the speaker. I often use a wireless clip-on microphone when addressing a group. This frees my hands for gestures, and also allows me to talk around and interact with the audience.

You can give two basic types of gestures: *demonstrative* and *emphatic.*

If you're self-conscious about gestures, start with demonstrative gestures. These are gestures that illustrate your words. If your sales staff came within 0.1 percent of reaching its goal, you can illustrate by holding your thumb and pointing finger a fraction of an inch apart and saying, "We missed it by that much." If you're describing the amount of paper work it takes to file your corporate taxes, you can hold your hand palm-down above your head and say "It takes a stack that high." You can also use demonstrative gestures to point directions.

As you practice, make sure that your gestures coincide with your words. If the gesture comes before or after the point you're making, it can confuse your listeners. A politician once gave a speech in which he roundly condemned those who advocated a proposal that was contrary to the interests of his constituents. But each time he referred to "they," he pointed to himself and when he referred to "we" he pointed elsewhere. His gestures told the audience that he was with "them"—the enemy.

After you feel comfortable with demonstrative gestures, begin working in some emphatic gestures. These are gestures designed to punctuate your speech. You might make a sweeping, outward movement of the hand, palm opened inward, as you explain a point. You might make the same motion with palm opened outward, to indicate a flat denial or rejection of an idea. You might make a chopping motion, with fist closed, to indicate vigorous determination. You might extend both hands, palms up, in a pleading gesture. Practice emphatic gestures to add power and persuasion to your speech.

THE FACE AND EYES

The face and eyes are eloquent message conveyers. Someone has estimated that humans are capable of 20,000 different facial expressions.

The most pleasant, and usually the most advantageous, is a smile. A smile can be the little bit of sugar that helps the medicine go down. It is always more pleasant to deal with people who smile than with those who frown.

The psalmist tells us that the eye is "the light of the body." The unvoiced testimony it offers is often the most eloquent.

Most people interpret a firm, steady gaze as a sign of sincerity. Darting, shifty eyes are interpreted as signs of untrustworthiness. A quick wink can convey a secret message silently across a crowded room. A coquettish look can set a heart to fluttering.

The ability to look someone in the eye is a sign of high self-esteem. When children fib to their parents, they usually look at the floor. It's hard to have self-esteem while you're telling a lie.

Steady eye contact is also a sign of assertiveness. People who consistently avoid the eyes of those to whom they speak are inviting others to treat them as doormats.

A Baptist minister in Moscow once told an American reporter an interesting story about the Russian poet Evgeny Yevtushenko.

Visiting a wealthy American, the poet noticed a magnificent moose head mounted on the wall of the home.

"How could you bear to shoot such a magnificent animal?" Yevtushenko asked.

"It was easy," said his host. "He didn't look me in the eye. If he had looked me in the eye, I couldn't have shot him."

A word of caution, though: Different cultures respond to eye contact in different ways. A gaze that may seem friendly to an American may be considered intrusive by an Asian. More about that in Chapter Eleven.

Even in the American culture, steady eye contact can be overdone. Most people feel uncomfortable when they're the objects of fixed, steady gazes. The most effective eye contact consists of a relaxed, steady gaze that is broken off intermittently. A good way to develop this habit is to look at someone and slowly count (in your head!) to three. This is usually the appropriate length of time to sustain a gaze in one-on-one conversations.

Sometimes, angry conversation leads to mutual glares in which each party tries to outstare the other. Don't be led into this kind of contest. If you find your eyes locked in a stare with an angry person, it's okay to break contact first. In fact, one theory holds that the dominant person will break contact first, since the dominant person takes the lead in all things.

CLOTHING AND GROOMING

Among the first things people notice about you is the way you dress and the way you groom yourself.

Many highly creative people affect a casual indifference toward their personal appearance, but in reality, they are making a purposeful statement. They are saying, in effect, "I'm so good at what I do that I don't have to dress for success."

Henry David Thoreau was such a person.

"Beware of all enterprises that require new clothes," he wrote.

If you plan to spend your life in the seclusion of a place like Walden Pond, follow Thoreau's advice. If you want to make it on Wall Street or Main Street, pay careful attention to the clothes you wear and the visual impact you have on others.

When dressing for the business world, follow the standard advice: Dress for inclusion. Look at what the people one or two steps up the corporate ladder from you are wearing and be guided by their tastes.

That's about the closest thing to universal advice that can be given in the realm of dress. Fads and fashions come and go, and what's in today may be passe tomorrow. And the fabric of American culture is quite varied. String ties and cowboy boots for men may be perfectly acceptable business attire in Fort Worth, but they would mark you as eccentric in Boston. Three-piece pinstripes may be the uniform of the day on Wall Street, but may be considered a bit stuffy on Hollywood Boulevard. And if that's true of America, it's even truer of other parts of the world. Wherever you are—in London or Sydney, in Singapore or Luxembourg—follow the fashion lead of the successful people in your business.

The perennial choice for the businessman in the industrialized nations is the gray or blue suit, with lighter shades in warm weather, darker ones in cool weather. Muted pinstripes seem never to go out of style. Brown suits are generally regarded as less authoritative than blue or gray ones.

Women have greater latitude for individuality in fashions, but the general rule still applies. In most businesses, it's best to avoid extremes. Seductive or coquettish outfits may draw admiring stares, but they won't enhance your reputation as a businesswoman.

Solid colors in women's clothing convey a message of seriousness and character. Plaids and prints are more whimsical. In the business office, successful women may be seen wearing suits, dresses, coordinates, and skirts with blazers. Different colors flatter different women. Find your best colors and stick with them.

Shoes should always be shined and in good repair. Adlai Stevenson, the American statesman, may be remembered for the famous photograph showing the hole in the sole of his shoe. But he is also remembered as the loser of two presidential elections.

If your job calls for a briefcase, invest in top-quality. It will contribute strongly to your image of success. If you need to have a pen in your breast pocket, make it a high-quality and attractive one. Avoid cheap plastic pens, and never wear pocket liners for pens.

Dress for Supervisors

The 21st century is ushering in an interesting development in dress for supervisors of blue-collar personnel. In the authoritarian work place, the difference between first-line supervisors and those who reported to them was usually marked by the presence or absence of neck ties. Women supervisors were likely to wear suits as opposed to dresses or slacks. A business suit was a symbol of status and authority. In companies that stress participative management, supervisors and team leaders usually dress in the same fashion as line workers. This implies to the workers that their supervisors are working with them, not over them.

For men, beards are a matter of taste. Make up your mind whether you want one. Don't go around looking as if you've forgotten to shave for the past couple of days. It may work for a Hollywood actor or the leader of a stateless people, but not for your average member of the corporate team. If you choose to wear a beard, keep it neatly trimmed.

Both men and women should avoid extremes of hair style. Again, use the look cultivated by the most successful people in your field as a guide, and adapt it to your own physical features.

THE FRIENDLY TOUCH

Jim Tunney, a close friend and colleague whom you've known for years as NFL Referee #32, is an eloquent advocate of participative management. He puts great emphasis on one other type of nonverbal communication: the touch of friendship and love.

We are all familiar with the need of children for touching and snuggling. Babies who never feel the loving touch of an adult have been known to die from inattention.

Adults too have this need. Tunney, who served for many years as a school headmaster, calls attention to the effects of beta endorphins. These are substances produced by the body that work on the same segments of the brain as morphine. They kill pain and elevate the mood.

Some people have systems that produce an ample supply of beta endorphins, so they have a built-in source of good feelings. If you were reared in a comfortable home by supportive parents, and especially if you are the oldest child, chances are you have a good built-in supply of beta endorphins.

That's because hugging, cuddling and other physical signs of affection stimulate the production of beta endorphins. Children who receive this kind of attention develop the ability to produce beta endorphins, and this morale-producing capacity stays with them.

Children who are not so fortunate grow up with a limited capacity for generating beta endorphins. They need outside help.

I'm not encouraging supervisors to engage in on-the-job hugging and cuddling. But friendly physical contact can be a great morale-booster. The occasional pat on the back or slap on the shoulder, or just a sympathetic touch on the arm can help create a sense of loyalty and affection that will pay dividends in quality and productivity on the job.

GIVING COMMUNICATION ANOTHER DIMENSION

The human brain has a unique capacity to form and recognize words, whether they're spoken or written. It also has the ability to send and understand messages through many other media.

Non-verbal language helps us to provide dimension to our communication. It supplies feelings to the raw words. The person who learns the art of communication in all its dimensions will have a powerful advantage in the business world of the 21st century.

Part Two of this book will explore work-place communication. Chapter Seven will look at ways management can encourage top-down, bottom-up and lateral communication throughout the organization.

PART TWO

Communicating in the Work Place

CHAPTER

7

Up, Down, and Across

In the early 20th century, lines of communication were neat and clean. Executives told subordinates what they wanted done. Subordinates either carried out their bosses' wishes or delegated them to people below. If the boss wanted information from down below, he asked for it. Communication followed a vertical channel, and most messages flowed from the top down.

The 21st century business will be an informational sponge that takes in information through countless pores, spreads it throughout the corporate body and pours it out where it does the most good.

Information will no longer just flow downward from the executive suite and upward through well-defined channels carved through layers of supervision. It will spread:

♦ From top management down to the employees.
♦ From employees upward to top management.
♦ Horizontally among all individuals and departments within the organization.

This up, down, and across communication will distinguish the thinking organization of the 21st century from the mechanistic organization of the 20th century.

FORMAL AND INFORMAL FUNCTIONS

Every organization has formal and informal information systems. The company can control the content, channels and direction of information through formal systems. Informal systems follow their own dynamics, mostly beyond the control of management or anyone else. Informal systems are also called "the grapevine."

More than half the information in an organization travels by grapevine. In some organizations, employees get 85% of their information from this informal source. Much of what they hear is accurate, but information from the grapevine is rarely complete. Surveys have shown that most employees prefer to get their information from official sources such as their supervisors, bulletin boards or the company newspaper.

The grapevine functions by default when management fails to provide full and accurate information through formal channels. Management has the opportunity to promote formal informational channels in upward, downward and horizontal directions.

TOP-DOWN COMMUNICATION

Top-down communication has traditionally been used to pass along instructions, to inform employees about policies and procedures, to rally them behind causes that management wishes to promote, and to let them know how their performance stacks up against the company's norm.

But 21st century employees aren't just looking to management for directions on what to do. They want to know *what* the company is doing and *how* the company is doing. They want to know how they can help the company and how the company can benefit them.

Here are some of the things the 21st century company might tell its employees through top-down communication:

♦ What products the company is producing and how they stack up to the competition.

- What kinds of benefits the company offers and how the employee can take advantage of them.
- What kind of future the company envisions and how it expects to achieve its vision.
- How the company is doing financially.
- What the company does with its earnings.
- How employees can improve their productivity.
- What advancement opportunities the company offers.
- What personnel policies and practices are in effect.
- What personnel changes have been made.
- What community activities the company is involved in.
- How the company stands on current issues.

One way of finding out what your employees want to know is to ask them. Conduct a survey to determine what they want you to tell them that you're not telling them now. Ask them where they now get their information about the company and where they'd like to get it.

OPTIONS FOR TOP-DOWN COMMUNICATION

Modern management has a wide range of options for top-down communication. Here are some of them:

- *Company newsletters.*

Advances in desktop publishing make newsletters technically feasible for almost any company. All you need is a word processor and a printer. Newsletters can be as elaborate or as simple as you want to make them, but always informative and enlightening.

The person ultimately responsible for it must have quick and easy access to top management. The newsletter should contain information that will be interesting and useful to employees, and should be part of a planned communications program.

♦ *Company newspapers and magazines.*

Newspapers and magazines are more elaborate than newsletters. They may require a full-time editor, depending upon how large you want to make it and how frequently you publish it. The newspaper can be an excellent vehicle for up, down and across communication, especially if it is produced under the direction of a communications professional. The editor should have ready access to top management as well as extensive contacts with people throughout the organization.

Newspapers and magazines usually are printed outside the company, although advances in desktop publishing technology make in-house printing feasible for many companies. Stew Leonard, who has won nationwide recognition for his management practices at his Connecticut dairy store, makes extensive use of employee publications. He found that the computerized equipment he acquired to print his store signs could be used to print an in-house magazine. His people produce a weekly newspaper, *Stew's Hotline,* and a magazine, *Stew's News,* that appears every two months.

My client, INA Bearing Company, has a superb magazine that captures employees' attention with personal information as well as subjects of universal interest. The magazine is aptly called "The Rolling Element." INA is the world's largest manufacturer of needle bearings, and "rolling element" describes the key component of a needle bearing.

♦ *Annual reports.*

If you use your annual report only as a tool for communicating statistical data to shareholders and other outside stakeholders, you're missing a good bet. Progressive companies today make effective use of photographs—of employees producing the products, of consumers using them, and of top executives interacting with the people they lead. In addition to providing statistics on financial performance, they promote corporate philosophy, goals, visions and missions.

They can be vehicles for communicating information about the company's products, long-range plans and financial progress.

A professionally produced annual report can promote enormous pride among employees by emphasizing the tangible and the intangible results of their efforts during the year. Why not consider a video cassette version of your annual report that can be shown to employees and made available to them for home viewing?

♦ *Employee handbooks.*

An employee handbook can be a valuable source of information on employee benefits and company policies. The handbook should be written for quick and easy comprehension. Steer clear of bureaucratic terms. Make sure company policies are stated clearly and unambiguously. Explain benefits such as health care and retirement plans in terms the average employee can understand without resorting to a dictionary. A loose-leaf format will allow for regular and inexpensive updating. A video cassette version of the handbook can also be a valuable orientation tool for new employees.

♦ *Bulletin boards.*

Strategically placed bulletin boards can provide a quick and inexpensive communications medium. Communications placed on the board should be printed or neatly typed. Many word-processor software programs provide a variety of type faces and sizes that can be used to produce attention-getting notices. The human-resources department can serve as the conduit through which management passes its messages to the bulletin board.

♦ *Inter-Office Memos.*

A survey of General Tire employees during the '80s showed that 44% of them preferred to receive information from management via interoffice memo. A memo enables you to target your message to the individual or group you want to reach, and to tailor it to the individuals and circumstances. To be effective, memos should be brief and to the point.

♦ *Letters.*

One of the most often-overlooked avenues for communication is the letter to employees' homes. When you send information into their homes, you reach employees at times and places that allow them to take time to look over the material without worrying about their on-the-job duties. It also makes it easier for them to share pertinent information with their families. Commendations sent to the home can be great morale-boosters.

♦ *Small group meetings.*

Many executives find it helpful to meet with employees in small groups to share information and concerns. Some hold quarterly or semi-annual meetings in which they tell employees how the company is doing financially and what changes, if any, are being contemplated.

One of my clients is Long Drug Stores, a West Coast chain of more than 300 stores that tops $3 billion in annual sales. The store, founded in 1938 by two brothers, Joe and Tom Long, is now run by Joe's son, Bob. Bob Long achieves two-way communications with his employees by holding regional town meetings.

The town-meeting concept can be used effectively as an avenue for two-way communication. Not only does it give management a chance to talk to employees; it can also give employees a chance to talk to management in a non-threatening atmosphere. Make it clear that employees are free to speak out on any topic that turns them on. If they voice complaints, address their concerns on the spot if possible. If that's not possible, assure them that you will look into what's bothering them and get back with them as soon as possible. Then keep your word!

♦ *Executive Speeches.*

When employees hear it directly from the CEO's mouth, it gives the message an extra measure of credibility. The CEO can find many occasions during the year to speak directly to employees. Awards banquets, holiday parties and other special events provide such opportunities. Too often, executives use these occasions to wave to the crowd, utter a few platitudes, and sit down.

Each time you have the opportunity to speak to a group of employees, think carefully about the message you want to present to them. Think about what the company stands for, what kind of future it envisions, and what it will take on the part of the employees to achieve that future. Then think of what you can say that will provide the employees with the information, the encouragement and the inspiration to give what it takes.

Executives often speak to local business, civic and community groups and at professional gatherings across the country. Sometimes these speeches are covered by the local media, but often the words don't carry beyond the room in which they are uttered. General Motors publishes an "Issues Update," consisting of excerpts on selected subjects from executive speeches. It mails it bimonthly to local communicators and members of management. Smaller companies don't have to produce separate publications for such material, but they can reproduce comments in the company newspaper or, on occasion, distribute copies of speeches to all employees or to key personnel.

EMPOWERMENT, NOT CONTROL

Remember that the purpose of top-down communications in the 21st century is to empower, not to control. Control limits possibilities. Empowerment expands possibilities. When you communicate *instructions* to your employees, you are limiting their latitude to respond. When you communicate *information,* you are expanding their latitude to respond. The 21st century corporation needs to be able to respond quickly and flexibly to fast-developing market situations. Therefore, employees at all levels need to know what products the company produces, what products they're competing with in the marketplace, and what they need to do to make their products competitive, if not superior.

Can you imagine a basketball coach taking a team into the second half without letting the players know the score, the identities and weaknesses of the opposing players, the number of personal fouls against them, or the amount of time remaining on the clock? Suppose the players hadn't been told that this game would determine whether they made it into the championship tournament. If the opposing team were minimally competitive, it probably would win the game.

Your employees need comparable information if they're to win in the arena of the marketplace.

UPWARD COMMUNICATION EMPOWERS MANAGEMENT

Top-down communication empowers your employees. Upward communication empowers management by keeping it informed of what's happening on the work floor and in the marketplace.

The first people to know about market trends are the people who make the sales to the ultimate consumer. The first people to know about technical defects in a product are the people who have to make the repairs or handle the complaints. The first people to hear about employee morale problems are the first-line supervisors. These people usually are far down on the corporate charts. What they know may make or break a company. Management needs to provide a way for them to be heard.

GE ERASES BOUNDARIES

At General Electric, CEO John F. Welch developed the concept of the "boundaryless corporation," in which information could flow freely up, down and across the corporate structure. Welch looked for barriers to communication, and when he found them he demolished them.

If you look around, you'll probably find plenty of boundaries in your own company that need to be removed. One of them may be the door to your office that remains closed to input from your employees. Executives who wall themselves off from the people they lead are depriving themselves of eyes and ears. If the people in your organization have to run an obstacle course of receptionists and secretaries to get into your presence or to gain your ear, you're not going to hear much from them. And what you don't know can hurt you.

Another barrier to upward communication is labeled "NIH," for "Not Invented Here."

Hardly a week goes by that my consulting work doesn't take me into a situation in which a company is suffering from the NIH syndrome. Some corporate cultures are hostile to ideas that don't originate in-house. You've heard of "the right way, the wrong way and the company's way." To paraphrase Vince Lombardi, in many organizations, the company's way isn't the best way; it's the only way. Salespeople, engineers, customer service reps and others operate at the meeting point of products and customers. They often pick up new ideas from competitors, suppliers, customers and other sources that their bosses don't encounter. When they bring these ideas home to your company, do the top executives listen to them or turn a deaf ear?

If your attitude is "If we didn't invent it, it ain't worth inventing," then you're shutting out a world of innovative ideas.

AN OUTSIDE IDEA WORTH $200 MILLION A YEAR

Because GE was receptive to ideas from beyond its corporate walls, it was able to reduce its average inventory levels by $200 million a year. Here's what happened:

Someone from GE discovered an appliance company in New

Zealand using an innovative method of compressing product cycle times. The idea was brought back to GE management, who put the method through a trial run in a Canadian affiliate, then transferred it to its largest appliance complex in Louisville, Kentucky. The method, which GE dubbed "Quick Response," enabled GE to respond more quickly to customer needs.

But GE didn't just introduce it in Louisville and forget it. It brought people in from each of its major businesses to study the method and adapt it to their own operations.

GE also dispatched people to Wal-Mart to learn about the management practices that propelled that business to the forefront in retailing.

GE management not only *listened* to ideas brought in by its people; it sent them out *looking* for ideas.

STIFLING LAYERS

Too many layers of management can stifle upward communications. If every communication has to "go through channels" and those channels must wind and twist through a dozen or more levels of responsibility, the chances of a message's surviving the trip undistorted are slim to none.

Generally speaking, a corporation should be able to function at peak efficiency with only five layers of management from line worker to CEO. Anything above that turns to fat instead of muscle.

In the old days, management provided people with upward mobility by giving them raises and titles. Soon the corporate work place was overrun by people with "manager" in their titles and no clear functions other than bottling up ideas and information in petty fiefdoms.

Some years ago I was called to a midwestern company that was choking on functionless functionaries. Interviews coupled with a needs analysis identified the problem. Despite considerable resistence, the company reorganized and cut out unnecessary titles. Individuals who were not performing functions that contributed to the corporate mission were reassigned to meaningful roles. Today, the company is much more fluid, fluent and profitable.

Look at your own work place. How many of your "managers" really need to manage? If you review the job titles and job descriptions in your company, you may see opportunities to reduce the number of management positions by replacing functionaries with leaders. If you do this, you'll be amazed at the way boundaries of authority can be turned into avenues of cooperation.

CROSS TRAINING ENCOURAGES COMMUNICATION

Too many specialized task functions also can impede the upward flow of information. If people are trained to do their own narrowly defined jobs, they have little understanding of the overall corporate process. Therefore, they might not recognize and pass along information that might be highly beneficial to management. As we go deeper into the 21st century, more workers will be educated to acquire several different job skills so that they will have broader understandings of where they fit into the total process.

Another factor that impedes upward communication is the Polyanna syndrome. Polyanna was the girl of fiction who refused to see the negative side of anything. It's a charming story, but the "see no evil" attitude can be deadly in the corporate setting. Executives need to know the bad news. Otherwise, how can they possibly deal with the negatives and overcome them? The way you encourage employees to bring you the bad news is to make it clear that you will listen and will do something about it.

The way to make sure you never hear any bad news is to implement the "kill-the-messenger" policy. If you punish the person who tells you there's a bridge out up ahead, the next time there's a bridge out you'll learn about it when you feel the water rising above your ears.

POSITIVE ENCOURAGEMENT OF UPWARD COMMUNICATION

It isn't enough to eliminate barriers to upward communication. Management also needs to set up systems that positively encourage such communication.

The traditional suggestion box is one such system. When you allow employees to submit anonymous questions, you free them from the inhibitions that accompany more open forms of communication. But if you allow the suggestion box to degenerate into a dead-letter file, you'll do more harm than good. Executives who invite people to put their complaints into a suggestion box should read the complaints, let the people know that they've read them, and tell them what, if anything, can be done about it.

W & J Rives, an apparel-manufacturing client of mine, uses its suggestion box to obtain feedback from employees. It rewards those who provide it with useful feedback, and where possible, communicates its responses back to the employees.

One way of letting people know that their suggestions are being read is to publish a column on them in the company newspaper or newsletter. The CEO could use this column to address specific suggestions or, if suggestions are too numerous, to summarize them and comment on the more interesting ones.

COMMUNICATING ACROSS THE CHART

Communicating across the corporate chart is a relatively new concept in business. In the past, management has forfeited this function to the grape vine.

Now, business leaders are beginning to realize the importance of cross-functional communication. A large diversified company may consist of several business units operating, essentially, as separate enterprises. But each unit probably has expertise that could be profitably shared with others. Each has probably developed sales, marketing and management techniques other units could beneficially adopt.

So corporate management should look for ways to incorporate the benefits of unity while exploiting the advantages of diversity.

One way to do this is to move personnel across divisional lines. This can provide your leaders and potential leaders with fresh perspectives, and your management team with hybrid vigor. People who deal with the challenges of different divisions of the company will develop corporate mentalities instead of a departmental mentalities.

UNITY IN DIVERSITY AT THE TEAM LEVEL

The principle of unity in diversity can be practiced all the way down to the team level. If everyone on a work team learns to do several jobs instead of specializing, the team develops a capacity for internal dialogue that can be of tremendous help in solving problems.

The rigid lines between salaried and non-salaried employees can block lateral communications. Just as a seasoned sergeant or chief petty officer can often impart useful advice and knowledge to a freshly commissioned officer, so veteran line workers can provide valuable insights to engineers, technicians and managers. Ask the engineer who worked with tool-and-die maker Charlie Dygert on that project at General Motors.

THE BOSS TAKES A BACK SEAT

Cross-functional teams require and encourage lateral communication. Such teams can be created to address problems and challenges that involve more than one function or department. Ford put together such a team to design the Taurus/Sable automobile. Levi Strauss used one to study the balance between work and family commitments. Chairman of the Board Robert Haas himself served on that task force, but only as a member.

"I'm on the task force, but I don't run it," he told the *Harvard Business Review.* "We have everyone from secretaries and sewing-machine operators to senior managers on the task force."[1] Haas realized that these line workers knew far more about the impact of their jobs on their family lives than he could possibly know as their CEO.

When people serve on cross-functional teams, they should answer to the team leader and not to the department from which they were drawn. Their performance should be evaluated on the basis of their contribution to the team effort and not on their contributions to their own department.

WAYS TO ENCOURAGE LATERAL COMMUNICATION

If teams are to function effectively, employees must feel free to communicate with anyone who can provide useful information without checking with higher authority. The old concept of "going through channels" has to be scrapped. If a team that assembles radios finds a pattern of defective parts from a supplier, it should feel free to contact the supplier and work out the problem without checking with department heads and vice presidents.

USING CORPORATE MEDIA

Management can also encourage lateral communications by providing media through which employees can get to know one another.

Many a client's employees have lamented to me over the years that "Things have changed around here. We've lost our personal touch; we're too big. At one time the president knew everyone by first name. Now the company is no longer a family. It's a big business."

The CEO of a large company can't know thousands of employees personally, and the employees can't all be in close personal touch with one another. But company publications can promote a family-like feeling throughout the company.

A company newspaper or magazine does not have to be strictly a tool for top-down communication. It can be a source of general information about the company and its people.

In addition to learning about what the company is doing and how it is doing, employees also want to know what and how their fellow employees are doing. Human-interest feature stories in company newspapers provide this kind of information. News of births, birthdays, weddings and anniversaries are well read and help promote a sense of community that encourages lateral communication.

An effective company newspaper looks at the company's stakeholders the way a general-circulation newspaper looks at the community it serves. It provides people with the information they need and desire, and it seeks, through communication, to provide a sense of community spirit.

Stew Leonard launched his weekly *Stew's Hotline* as a six- to eight-page publication full of stories and photographs about store employees and their activities. He used his store's own printer. The photographs were usually made with instant-developing cameras so that the activities could be recognized while they were still fresh. Stew also inaugurated a bi-monthly magazine, *Stew's News,* insisting that no issue go to press until it had 200 photographs of employees.

THE FOUR F's REQUIRE GOOD COMMUNICATION

If a company is to prosper in the 21st century, then all barriers to the flow of information and ideas into and through the company must be removed.

Rosabeth Moss Kanter taught us that modern companies must observe the Four F's, by being focused, flexible, fast and friendly. You can't be any of those unless information can flow fast and freely from all corners of the organizations.

You can't focus the efforts of your entire work force if your organization is criss-crossed with walls that impede the flow of communication.

You can't be flexible if you have a rigid corporate structure in which every division and department is a closed information loop with no lines of communication to other parts of the organization. You can't respond to the market if you erect barriers to information flowing in from the outside.

You can't be fast if information has to seep slowly through layer after layer of management.

And you can't be friendly if your people don't talk to other people inside and outside your organization.

In the old days, everyone had to "go through channels," and only a handful of people had automatic access to the sending and receiving ends of the channels.

In the new business environment, the channels have to branch into an informational network that reaches every level and every corner of the organization. Not only must management be able to communicate with employees, but employees must be able to communicate with management and—just as importantly—with each other.

We have already learned that all communication is personal. Communication, reduced to its elemental components, consists of sending mutually comprehensible messages from one mind to another. That means that to become a truly effective leader and communicator, you must learn to communicate one-on-one.

Chapter 8 will explore this important aspect of communication.

Communicating One on One

Most of the verbal communicating you do is from one individual to another. This is true whether you're in a family, social, or a work setting.

"When you think about it, the only thing a manager does that is visible to the organization is to listen and speak, and to draw and interpret symbols," remarked Ray Stata, CEO of Analog Devices. "Speaking and listening are where it's at."[1]

One-on-one verbal communication affords the greatest opportunity for precision, because immediate feedback can tell you whether you were understood accurately.

But communicating effectively involves more than just accuracy. The purpose of most communication is to influence the attitudes and behaviors of those whom we address. Since the human race is composed of billions of individuals, each with a different way of responding, no one approach is universally effective. So it's important that you learn to express yourself accurately and in a way that will accomplish your purpose toward the individual you're addressing.

THE BASIC PROCESS OF COMMUNICATING

To achieve precision and effectiveness in communicating, you should understand the basic process of communication. It has four requirements:

♦ A message must be conveyed.
♦ The message must be received.
♦ There must be a response.
♦ Each message must be understood.

Let's look at these requirements one at a time.

A MESSAGE MUST BE CONVEYED

That sounds simple enough. You know what your thoughts are, and you know how to translate them into words. But that's where we lose the simplicity.

Each of us has our own mental dialect. It is the common language of the culture in which we grow up, modified by our own unique life's experiences. Our life's experiences add color and shades of meaning to different words.

When you speak, your mental dialect must be translated into the mental dialect of the hearer. So the words you speak acquire a different color when they pass through the ears of the person who hears you.

Spook or Spirit?

Dr. Muriel O'Tuel, a South Carolina educator with whom I have worked, once told of the time her young son, Bryant, balked at staying overnight with his grandparents, whom he had always dearly loved.

Asked why, he responded, "I'm afraid of the ghost."

Dr. O'Tuel was mystified. She had grown up in her parents' home and had never seen or heard anything that looked or sounded like a spook.

Some gentle inquiry revealed the source of Bryant's apprehension. He had accompanied his grandparents to church one Sunday, and the sermon had revolved around the Holy Ghost. In the church the O'Tuels attended, the reference usually was to the Holy Spirit. So in Bryant's mental dialect, "Holy Ghost" had a meaning quite different from the one his parents and grandparents understood.

A Cut from the Morgue

Old-time newspaper people tell about the young copy boy who quit after his first day on the job. The mayor had died in an automobile accident, and the editor had told the young man, "Go down to the morgue and get us a cut of the mayor." The copy boy hadn't learned that in the newspaper parlance of the day, "the morgue" referred to the newspaper's own reference library, and that a "cut" was no more than an engraving of the mayor's photograph, which the newspaper kept on file for quick use whenever the mayor made news. What, in the sender's mental dialect, was a perfectly reasonable and routine request was, in the receiver's dialect, a macabre and perverted demand.

It Depends Upon Where You Are

You can probably think of numerous opportunities for misunderstandings on your job and in your culture. If you tell your travel agent you want a flight to Portland, be sure to specify Maine or Oregon. Otherwise, you may end up on the wrong coast. A colleague of mine once flew to Ohio to keep a speaking engagement in Columbus. Too late, he realized that the group he was to address was in Columbus, Georgia. If someone in my hometown of High Point, North Carolina asks me, "How did Carolina do in the big game last night?" I know the reference is to the Tar Heels of the University of North Carolina. If somebody in Columbia puts the question in those precise words, I know that "Carolina" means the Gamecocks of the University of South Carolina. In most cities, if you ask a newsstand operator for the Sunday Times, you'll be handed a New York Times. But in St. Petersburg, Florida, or Seattle, Washington, you're likely to get the local newspaper.

Synchronize Your Vocabularies

When communicating in the work place, be sure that you and the people with whom you communicate are working with the same set of words and meanings. Adjust your vocabulary to the vocabulary of the person with whom you're speaking. And say *exactly* what you mean. In modern speech, we often let our sentences trail off into an expression such as "you know," and "stuff like that." This leaves it up to the hearer to supply the meaning. Your meaning may be quite obvious to you. But if the listener is on a different wave length, it may be quite different.

THE MESSAGE MUST BE RECEIVED

The second basic requirement of the one-on-one communication process is that the message be received and understood. Effective communicators know that they have not conveyed their meaning until they have made sure that the other person has received it exactly as they sent it. They test, with questions and observations, to make sure that the real meaning they wanted to convey has passed through the filters and has been received and understood.

A Dance That Was Tutu Naughty for Church

One businessman neglected to seek the proper feedback when he approached the pastor of his church, and the result was severe embarrassment.

The businessman was looking for ways to raise money for the church softball team, and he approached the pastor.

"Some friends of mine told me about a dancer who is drawing big crowds around the country, and I thought we might bring her here for a benefit performance," he said. "Would you object to a belly dancer for a fund-raiser?"

"Of course not," said the pastor. "Go ahead and use the church's Fellowship Hall if you'd like."

So the businessman arranged for the performance and the pastor was on hand for the show. When the dancer came on stage and began her seductive gyrations, the pastor gasped and turned to the businessman.

"How *could* you bring an act like this into the church?"

"But you said it was all right to bring in a belly dancer," the businessman said.

"*Belly* dancer?" said the pastor. "I thought you said *ballet* dancer!"

A few follow-up questions during the initial conversation would have averted this scene. The pastor's unhesitating assent should have thrown up a red flag in the businessman's mind.

"Do you know what a belly dancer does?" he might have asked. Or "I'm told there's nothing lewd about the act, but the dancer will be wearing filmy clothes and she may make some suggestive moves. Do you feel comfortable with that?"

Feedback Is Vital on the Job

In the business world, too, feedback is important. Serving on the board of the Economic Development Corporation for the city of High Point, I've learned to nail down every detail when major real-estate transactions are involved. Let's say that you're a developer considering two parcels of land for an office park. So you tell your representative: "Let's go with the parcel on the west end, provided the city is willing to extend water and sewer mains to the perimeter and assume responsibility for maintenance of internal streets and sidewalks. If the city agrees to the utilities but refuses to take over street maintenance, let's try for a relaxation of parking requirements and try to get the purchase price down by 10%. If that's impossible, we'll have to opt for the Northside tract."

Before your representative goes out the door, briefcase in hand, you'd better get her to repeat those conditions. Otherwise, you may become the victim of crossed signals and end up with the wrong parcel of land.

Ask Your Listener to Paraphrase

The best kind of feedback is a paraphrased version of your message. Paraphrasing converts the message into your hearer's mental dialect and reflects it back to you. You now have a chance to hear the message the way your hearer received it. You can compare what you hear with what you said, and the two of you can reflect the message back and forth until you're sure that mutual understanding has occurred.

THERE MUST BE A RESPONSE

The goal of all communication is to obtain the desired response. You want to say something correctly, and have your hearer understand what you mean by it. But you also want the hearer to do something in response.

The Assertive Approach

Good one-on-one communication calls for an assertive approach. That means letting your hearers know clearly, unambiguously and courteously what you expect of them as a result of the communication.

Assertive messages make use of the pronoun "I." When you say "You ought to make at least three sales calls per day," you're giving the hearer an "out." "Ought" doesn't mean "must," and your hearer may respond with "Yes, but . . ."

When you say "I would like for you to make at least three sales calls per day," you make clear what your expectations are.

Focus on the Behavior, Not on the Individual

When you want to modify someone's behavior, it's important that your message focus on the behavior and not on the individual. It does no good to say, "Bill, you're careless and slovenly and you're going to have to shape up or ship out." Such a message is demoralizing to Bill and gives him no guidelines for meeting your expectations.

A good assertive message begins by describing the specific behavior that you find unsatisfactory. Then it describes the effects that behavior has on you and others in your organization. Finally, it describes the behavior you desire.

So you might take this approach with Bill:

> *Bill, I've noticed recently that you're waiting until the last minute to figure your estimates, and they're coming to me with significant errors. I caught a couple this month that could have cost the company thousands of dollars. When your estimates are done hastily, I have to go over them line by line, which is a serious drain on my time. I would like for you to organize your time so that you don't have to do your estimates in a hurry. And I want you to go over them twice, double-checking all data, before turning them in to me.*

Using this approach, you're not accusing Bill of being careless or slovenly. You're focusing on his behavior, using objective information. And you're telling him clearly what changes you want him to make. Notice, though, that you're not issuing a command. "I would like" and "I want" are quite different from "you must."

A couple of other suggestions: Don't dwell on the past. You can't change yesterday's behavior. You can only aim for the future. And be specific.

Four Basic Behavior Patterns

Be aware, too, that people respond to your words in different ways. Good leaders learn the behavior styles of the people they lead and adjust their approaches accordingly.

If you observe carefully, you'll find that people fall into one or another of these broad categories:

♦ **Dominators.**

These are your fierce competitors. They are pragmatic, decisive, and intent on winning. When you approach them, forget the small talk. They want you to get to the point. They're not interested in minor details. Give them the big picture. They want to know *how* something works, and not *why* it works that way. Be direct and assertive with them. They don't respond to hints. They're likely to challenge you, and if you yield they'll exploit the advantage. Stand your ground and they'll respect you. Dominators don't like to be manipulated, so always be straightforward with them. When you compliment them, praise their achievements and not their personal qualities; Dominators don't want to appear soft. When you discuss problems with them, let them be part of the solution.

♦ **Interactors.**

Interactors are the most sociable of the behavior types. They like to interact with people, and they bask in the admiration of others. They're the people who will know everyone by first name. Like Dominators, they prefer the big picture to minute details, but small talk is fine with them. They respond to pep talks more readily than the other behavior types do.

Interactors want to be included in whatever is going on. They don't like to work in isolation. They enjoy compliments and are devastated by public criticism. With them it is especially important that you follow the rule: "Praise in public, criticize in private." But make sure the compliment is sincere. They recognize and resent insincere praise.

Approach them in a friendly manner, and be aware of your body language. Interactors are very sensitive to non-verbal clues. They'd rather communicate by conversation than by memo, but they have short memories for detail. When you reach an agreement with them, nail it down in writing.

When you're teaching them, give them an outline, a timetable or a step-by-step procedure and hold them to it. Interac-

100

tors like to ad lib, and often overestimate their own competence.

♦ *Relaters.*

Relaters are known for their steadiness and their ability to work well with other behavior styles. They are less aggressive and less decisive than Dominators and Interactors, and prefer to make decisions by group consensus. Relaters dislike conflict and will go to great lengths to get along with others. In the process, they may suppress their own feelings. Relaters may think they're carrying an unfair portion of the work load, but they won't complain openly.

Relaters like comfortable, casual, low-key environments. Like the Interactors, they like to be on first-name terms with people. Whereas Interactors want to be liked and admired, Relaters want to be liked and appreciated. They are good listeners, and they are likely to adhere to procedures. They are uncomfortable with change.

When dealing with Relaters, assure them that they're highly valued. When changes are necessary, prepare them well in advance, and stress the factors that will remain unchanged. When it's necessary to criticize their behavior, reassure them of your high regard for them as persons.

♦ *Evaluaters.*

Evaluaters are drawn more to logic than to feelings. They are guided by inner standards, which they strive to meet, regardless of whether their efforts are applauded.

Evaluaters are the mirror images of Dominators. Whereas Dominators skip the details and cut to the big picture, Evaluaters revel in details. If you want somebody to maintain your aircraft or perform open-heart surgery, an evaluater is an excellent choice.

Whereas Dominators will try to expand their areas of responsibility, Evaluaters need to have their roles clearly defined.

Evaluaters are interested in how things work, whether they're dealing with mechanical devices or human systems. If you want to know what the rule book says, ask an evaluater. If you need help interpreting a computer manual, ask an evaluater.

Evaluaters are more interested in quality than in quantity. They're drawn more to reasoning than to imagination. Whereas Dominators and Interactors are action-oriented, Evaluaters are methodical perfectionists who won't commit to action until they're certain every detail has been nailed down.

When you communicate with them, skip the small talk. They're interested in practical matters. Don't waste your breath on pep talks. Just show them how to do a better job. Be very careful when you criticize their work. Evaluaters identify very closely with their performance, and when you criticize it you're criticizing them. Put the emphasis on the positive. Don't say, "Pat, I think your site plan is functional, but it falls flat esthetically." Instead, say "Pat, your site plan meets all the functional criteria. Let me make a few suggestions on esthetics." With this approach, you're not finding fault with Pat's plan; you're providing guidance in improving it. That's what the Evaluater is looking for.

Evaluaters share the Relater's lack of aggressiveness. They'll accumulate a rich store of information and will be glad to share it with others if they're asked. But you have to ask. They also share the Relater's aversion to conflict. Keep their environment free of turmoil.

Don't play semantic games with them. Be open and straightforward. When they ask questions, give direct answers. The evaluater is looking for information, not conversation.

EACH MESSAGE MUST BE UNDERSTOOD

Once a message has been delivered, received and responded to, it's time to take stock of what each person has communicated. The cycle of communication is complete only when you come away with a clearer understanding of the person with whom you sought to communicate. You may not always agree with the other person, and the other person may not always agree with you—but it is important that you understand each other.

Successful communicators learn to recognize and overcome barriers to communication. There are two types of such barriers: those arising from the environment and those stemming from the hearer's resistance.

Environmental Barriers

Those arising from the environment include:

♦ Distractions.
♦ Disturbances.
♦ Diversions.
♦ Discomfort.

If you've ever tried to talk with a friend at a crowded and noisy business party, you can readily understand how the environment can present major barriers. If you've ever tried to carry on a conversation in a room where a rock band was going full blast, you can appreciate the noise barrier.

A good general tries not to commit his troops on terrain that presents inherent disadvantages. Good communicators follow similar strategies. They try not to set up conversations in settings that will compete for attention.

If you're planning to discuss an important business transaction, don't do it over drinks in a noisy lounge. If you want to combine business with food and beverage, choose a quiet restaurant, club or cafe. If you're going to discuss personnel matters with a supervisor, don't do it on a noisy factory floor. Find a quiet office or conference room. If you're going to go over a set of complicated plans, don't spread them across a table beside a hotel pool. The distractions at a swimming pool may be pleasant, but they *are* distractions. I once spoke to a sales convention in a resort hotel where the meeting room had an open view of the pool. Most of the salespeople were men and the pool was populated with beautiful women wearing skimpy suits. It was hard enough for me to pay attention to what I was saying, and I can only imagine what the audience was going through. You can't really compete with that kind of distraction. Find a setting that will allow you to devote full attention to the agenda before you.

When you are communicating with an individual, that individual deserves your full attention. Choose a time and a place that will minimize interruptions. If you're meeting in your office during business hours, have your secretary hold telephone calls, or use your telephone answering device for the duration of the conversation. Many executives set aside certain times of day during which they will receive telephone calls and unscheduled visitors. The rest of the time, they reserve for creative thinking, strategic planning, decision-making and other duties of leadership.

When disturbances do occur, try not to talk over them. If the disturbance is obviously temporary, suspend the conversation until the interruption is past. If it's obviously going to be prolonged, try to reschedule the conversation for a more favorable time.

I often teach salespeople where to sit on sales calls or when they're conducting business over a meal. My advice: Put the other person's back to any distractions, so your listener's attention won't be constantly diverted by what's happening in the background.

Finally, pay attention to comfort. I've given more than 5,000 speeches and seminars, and I've battled all kinds of odds. I can tell you that audience discomfort is one barrier you can't overcome: your only winnable strategy is to avoid it. So stay away from settings that are too hot, too cold or otherwise uncomfortable. Nobody can concentrate while in a state of discomfort. And if the person you need to communicate with is ill, injured or going through some emotional trauma, it's best to reschedule the conversation. Otherwise, you're going up against impossible barriers to communication.

Monitoring the environment is the task of any person who wishes to communicate, whether as a company leader, a salesperson, a manager, or a letter writer. You just can't ignore such barriers. To do so is to give up and let the competing voices have your audience. If people are distracted or interrupted, or they feel uncomfortable, they're not likely to tune you in completely, understand your message thoroughly, or respond to you positively.

Audience Resistance

Barriers resulting from audience resistance fall into two categories: external factors that cause people to tune you out, and internal factors that prevent them from giving you their complete attention.

People often form first impressions on the basis of external factors. If the first impression is negative, you won't get the person's attention. Look for characteristics of dress, speech and actions that may be turning people off. If your dress is too casual, frivolous or distracting, you may be losing listeners. If your voice is strident, shrill or guttural, people may find you unpleasant to listen to. In certain areas, regional accents may turn people off. If you speak with a pronounced regional accent and are doing business in a region where that accent is not commonly heard, you may have to look for ways to overcome this barrier. You may want to work on acquiring a more generic accent. Or you may want to spend some time cultivating the person's confidence.

It goes without saying that good grooming and good personal hygiene are essential to good communication. Body odor, halitosis, or a disheveled appearance will cause people to turn away from you.

Internal Barriers

Internal barriers to communication may stem from a lack of interest in what you're saying or a lack of understanding.

If you discern a lack of interest, then your task is to find some way to lead your listener to identify with your message. How does it concern your listener personally? What bearing does it have on the listener's job, income, health, family, or security? Once you establish that point of identity, you'll have attention.

People have a way of erecting defense mechanisms and emotional barriers when they feel threatened by what you are saying or by the way you are saying it. Studies have repeatedly shown that people, like other creatures, feel protective of their territories. Invade those turfs, or act in a threatening manner, and you will be sure to turn off their attention. When your task is to deliver an unpleasant message or to persuade your listener to take some unpleasant action, look for ways to neutralize the negatives and to reassure the person who feels threatened.

Bonds of Misunderstanding

Sometimes, it's just a question of not understanding what you're talking about. During World War II, the United States raised money for defense by selling war bonds. In some remote parts of the country, where newspapers, radios and public schools had not yet penetrated, people were a little slow to learn about the heroic leadership of Winston Churchill, the Japanese sneak attack on Pearl Harbor and the determined response of Franklin Roosevelt.

So when a bond salesperson approached a farmer who was out in the barnyard slopping his hogs, the salesperson was frustrated at the lack of interest in his patriotic mission.

"Wouldn't you like to help out by buying some war bonds?" he asked.

"Reckon not," replied the farmer.

"Wouldn't you like to join the defense effort with Mr. Roosevelt?"

"Nope, reckon not."

"Aren't you upset over what they did to Pearl Harbor?"

"Reckon not."

"Don't you want to be on the side of Churchill?"

"Nope."

"So you don't want any bonds?"

"Nope."

Frustrated, the salesperson moved on.

The farmer's wife came over and asked who the stranger had been.

"Some fellow had a story about a guy named Roosevelt who got a woman named Pearl Harbor in trouble over on the side of Church Hill and wanted me to go his bond."

Sometimes, you have to explain very carefully.

KEEP IT SIMPLE

The most important thing you can do to make sure that you're understood is to keep your communication simple. People don't like to be led through a maze of words and mental meanderings before they reach the main point of your message.

Once while evangelist Billy Graham was flying into Dallas to address the student body of a large seminary, a storm moved in. Visibility at the airport became so low that his plane couldn't land. So it had to circle over the city for several hours—long beyond the time of his scheduled appearance. But no one on the ground knew that his plane couldn't land.

"It occurred to me while I was up there circling around," he later told a group, "that as preachers, we spend most of our time circling around in a fog, while people are wondering where in the world we are."

It's a condition that plagues people in any business. The high art of plain talk is simply saying something so that it can be understood. And it's the best way to clear away the fog from all your communication attempts. But how do you do it?

SIX COMMUNICATION TECHNIQUES

Here are six techniques I use to help me say things simply but persuasively, and even forcefully:

(1) *Get your thinking straight.* The most common source of confusing messages is muddled thinking. We have an idea we haven't thought through. Or we have so much we want to say that we can't possibly say it. Or we have an opinion that is so strong we can't keep it in. As a result, we are ill prepared when we speak, and we confuse everyone. The first rule of plain talk, then, is to think before you say anything. Organize your thoughts.

(2) *Say what you mean.* Say exactly what you mean.

(3) *Get to the point.* Effective communicators don't beat around the bush. If you want someone to buy something, ask for the order. If you want someone to do something, say exactly what you want done.

(4) *Be concise. Don't waste words.* Confusion grows in direct proportion to the number of words used. Speak plainly and briefly, using the shortest, most familiar words.

(5) *Be real.* Each of us has a personality—a blending of traits, thought patterns and mannerisms—which can aid us in communicating clearly. For maximum clarity, be natural, and let the real you come through. You'll be more convincing and much more comfortable.

(6) *Speak in images.* The cliche that "a picture is worth a thousand words" isn't exactly true (try explaining the Internal Revenue code using nothing but pictures). But words that help people visualize concepts can be tremendous aids in communicating a message. Once Ronald Reagan's Strategic Defense Initiative became known as Star Wars, its opponents had a powerful weapon against it. The name gave it the image of a far-out, futuristic dream beyond the reach of current technology. Reagan was never able to come up with a more powerful positive image.

Your one-on-one communication will acquire real power if you learn to send messages that are simple, clear, and assertive; if you learn to monitor the hearer to determine that your message was accurately received; and if you learn to obtain the desired response by approaching people with due regard for their behavioral styles.

Your finesse as a communicator will grow as you learn to identify and overcome the obstacles to communication. Practice the six techniques I just mentioned, and you'll find your effectiveness as a message-sender growing steadily.

But sending messages is only half the process of communicating. To be a truly accomplished communicator, you must also cultivate the art of listening.

If you're approaching a railroad crossing around a blind curve, you can send a message with your car horn. But that's not the most important part of your communication task. The communication that counts takes place when you stop, look and listen.

Chapter Nine will emphasize the listening aspect of communication.

CHAPTER 9

Stop, Look—and Listen

We're all familiar with the warning on the signs at railroad crossings: Stop, Look and Listen. It's also a useful admonition for communication.

It's easy to think of communication as a process of sending messages. But sending is only half the process. Receiving is the other half. So at the appropriate time, we have to stop sending and prepare to receive. As Marc Antony admonished the Romans in Shakespeare's *Julius Caesar,* "Be silent that you may hear."

A sign on the wall of Lyndon Johnson's Senate office expressed Antony's thought in a more down-to-earth way: "When you're talking, you ain't learning."

SOMETHING CLICKED

Many years ago, a young man went to a Western Union office to apply for a job as a telegrapher. In those days, messages were still transmitted in Morse Code through audible clicks.

The young man had no experience in telegraphy, but he had studied it at home, and he knew the code.

His heart sank as he walked into the office and looked over the crowd of people filling out application forms.

As he sat down with his own form, he heard a clicking noise in the background. He stopped filling out his form and listened. Then he dashed into the nearby office. Moments later, a man emerged and told the other applicants they could go home. The job had just been filled.

What got him the job?

The clicking noise was the sound of a telegraph receiver. The young man listened and translated the clicks into words: "If you understand this message, come into the office. The job is yours."

LISTENING PAYS

Listening pays off daily in the world of business. When you interview a candidate for a position with your company, you normally spend about 80% of your time listening. Smart salespeople have learned that you can talk your way out of a sale, but you can listen your way into one. They listen to their customers to find out what their needs are, then concentrate on filling those needs. Skilled negotiators know that no progress can be made until they have heard and understood what the other side wants. Enlightened employers listen to their employees and learn about their wants and needs.

LISTENING TO SAUSAGE GRINDERS

Ralph Sayer brought 21st century management into the world of sausage grinding as CEO of Johnsonville Foods in Sheboygan Falls, Wisconsin. Sayer became a strong believer in management by listening. He went out into his plants and opened his ears.

One of the complaints he heard was that new employees were poorly trained. This put a burden on the other employees, who had to rectify their mistakes and compensate for their low productivity.

"We gotta fix it," they told their CEO.

"You're absolutely right," Sayer responded, "and you guys know what these people need to know when they come in . . . Train them."

Sayer reasoned that the employees themselves knew more about the job requirements than the human-resources department did, so he put the employees in charge of hiring, firing and training.[1]

When his employees complained about co-workers who brought "boom boxes" into the plant and played the music loud, Sayer didn't tell them what to do. He asked them for solutions, and he listened.

I would replace the training element of Sayer's formula with a system of comprehensive, integrated employee education. This would provide his workers with the skills to meet their expanded responsibilities. But his willingness to listen to the people on the work floor is exemplary, and other executives would do well to emulate him.

LISTENING REQUIRES THOUGHT AND CARE

Listening, like speaking and writing, requires thought and care. If you don't concentrate on listening, you won't learn much, and you won't remember much of what you learn.

Some experts claim that professionals earn between 40% and 80% of their pay by listening. Yet, most of us retain only 25% of what we hear. If you can increase your retention and your comprehension, you can increase your effectiveness in the 21st century's Age of Information.

THE BENEFITS OF LISTENING

Skillful listening offers these benefits:

- ◆ You will learn from what you hear.
- ◆ You can show the people to whom you listen that you're interested in them.
- ◆ You can gain insight into the way others perceive their individual needs, desires and motivations.

- You give others a chance to let down their guards so that they can hear what you have to say.
- You can actively involve others in the communication process.
- You can clarify misconceptions.

LISTEN WITH YOUR EYES

If you listen only with your ears, you're missing out on much of the message. As we learned in Chapter Seven, some of the most important communication is done without words. Good listeners keep their eyes open while listening.

Look for feelings. The face is an eloquent communication medium. Learn to read its messages. While the speaker is delivering a verbal message, the face can be saying, "I'm serious," "Just kidding," "It pains me to be telling you this," or "This gives me great pleasure."

Some non-verbal signals to watch for:

- *Rubbing one eye.* When you hear "I guess you're right," and the speaker is rubbing one eye, guess again. Rubbing one eye often is a signal that the speaker is having trouble inwardly accepting something.
- *Tapping feet.* When a statement is accompanied by foot-tapping, it usually indicates a lack of confidence in what is being said. If a vendor says "We can deliver the goods within six weeks," while toes or heels are moving up and down, better allow for a couple of extra weeks.
- *Rubbing fingers.* When you see the thumb and forefinger rubbing together, it often means that the speaker is holding something back. It may be a signal for you to ask some penetrating questions.
- *Staring and blinking.* If you've made your best offer and the other person stares at the ceiling and blinks rapidly, your offer

is under consideration. Allow time for a decision to be made. If you hear a deep breath and a sigh, the decision has probably been made.

♦ *Crooked smiles.* As Shakespeare wrote, "One may smile, and smile and be a villain." Most genuine smiles are symmetrical. And most facial expressions are fleeting. If a smile is noticeably crooked or if it remains for more than a moment or two, you're probably looking at a fake smile, and you're quite possibly listening to an untruth.

♦ *Eyes that avoid contact.* Poor eye contact can be a sign of low self-esteem, but it can also indicate that the speaker is not being truthful. Most people find it hard to look you in the eye while lying to you. But before you judge a person's motives by eye contact, remember that in some cultures, direct eye contact is considered rude.

♦ *Forced eye contact.* Just as lack of eye contact can be a sign of lying, so forced eye contact can be a sign of faking it.

♦ *Frequent rubbing of the nose.* This can also signal a lack of candor.

It would be unwise to make a decision based solely on these visible signals. But they can give you valuable tips on the kind of questions to ask and the kind of answers to be alert for.

GOOD LISTENERS MAKE THINGS EASY

People who are poor listeners will find few who are willing to come to them with useful information.

"No one cares to speak to an unwilling listener," said Jerome, the scholar of the 4th and 5th centuries, who translated the Bible into Latin.

Good listeners make it easy on those to whom they want to listen. They make it clear that they're interested in what the other person has to say.

When you're ready to listen to someone, eliminate all the competition for your attention. Put aside whatever you've been working on. Listening can't be a part-time activity. Turn off the radio, television set or stereo. Assume an alert posture, facing the speaker squarely and at eye level. Show that you're ready to listen by leaning toward the speaker. Keep arms and legs uncrossed. Be respectful of the speaker's "bubble of space," positioning yourself neither too close nor to far away.

As the conversation proceeds, you can guide it with body language. A single nod keeps the conversation going. A double nod encourages the speaker to elaborate. A triple nod may make the speaker hesitate, change the subject, or gradually wind down.

A listener's verbal response can either ignite a conversation or squelch it. Figure 9–1 contains examples of igniter phrases and squelcher phrases.

MONOLOGUES IN DUET

Remember that conversation is an interactive process. In a truly productive conversation, two or more minds are engaged in a mutual enterprise: the interchange of thoughts. This process often degenerates into a monologue in duet: We're thinking about what we're about to say instead of listening to what the other person is saying. When we do that, we often miss out on key points or misunderstand what has been said.

The process of listening involves interpretation, evaluation and reaction. Listen carefully to what the other person is saying. Put yourself in the speaker's shoes and try to interpret what you hear from the speaker's point of view. What is the speaker thinking and feeling?

Fit what you hear into the framework of what you already know, and evaluate it against your present knowledge. Ask questions for clarification, and listen carefully to the answers. Then give your reaction.

I often use three exercises to demonstrate to audiences the value
of listening carefully and evaluating what is being said.

In one, I ask the audience to repeat the word "joke" each time I
hold up my hand.

IGNITERS	SQUELCHERS
I like that . . .	The problem with that is . . .
Keep talking, you're on track . . .	No way it will work here . . .
Go ahead, try it! . . .	Impossible under our current system . . .
We can do a lot with that idea . . .	It's not a bad idea, but . . .
That's great, how can we do it? . . .	We've never done it that way before . . .
That's neat! What else do we need? . . .	You haven't considered . . .
How can we get support for it? . . .	We have too many projects now . . .
I think it will fly . . .	It won't work . . .
Gee, why not? . . .	We haven't the time . . .
Hey, that's a great idea . . .	We're not ready for it yet . . .
How can we build on that idea? . . .	It's all right in theory, but not in practice . . .
I agree! . . .	Let's be practical . . .
How can we help you? . . .	Why start anything now? . . .
This is going to be fun! . . .	You know, I think you really are dumb . . .
I love challenges like this . . .	Has anyone else tried it? . . .
That would be interesting to try . . .	It's been the same for 10 years. Why change now? . . .

Figure 9–1

After they've responded with "joke" several times, I ask, "What do you call the white part of an egg?"

The audience invariably answers, "yolk." Which leaves me wondering what they would call the yellow part of an egg.

In another exercise, I begin by saying, "Imagine you are a bus driver and it is your mission to drive your bus due north four miles, due east three miles, due south two miles and due west one mile."

While my listeners are trying to track the bus's route in their minds, I ask the question: "How old is the bus driver."

Few people remember that I began by saying "Imagine *you* are a bus driver . . ."

In the third exercise, I ask the audience to give me a four-letter word beginning with *S* that describes what you do when you go to a mall.

That one's a piece of cake: ***Shop.***

Now, I say, give me a four-letter word starting with *S* that describes what you do when you return merchandise to exchange it for something else.

Most of the audience responds: ***Swap.***

Now (listen carefully), think of a word that describes what you do when you come to a green light.

If you said "Stop," you need to go back for a remedial driving course—or perhaps you need to take a course in listening.

Note that I didn't specify the number of letters in the last word, and I didn't say what letter it began with.

These are more than cute exercises designed to draw chuckles from an audience. They clearly illustrate the value of interpreting and evaluating before reacting to what you hear.

AWAIT YOUR TURN TO TALK

When you sit down to listen, don't try to seize the floor before the speaker is ready to yield—unless you are trapped in the presence of a non-stop talker and you have to interrupt in the interest of time.

Busy executives don't have to become captives of long-winded bores. When you find yourself in the presence of such a motor-mouth, you may have to break in at strategic points and try to keep the conversation focused.

But in normal conversations, the speaker will let you know when it's time for you to speak. The signal could come in the form of a question, an expectant look, or a pause that gives you a chance to step in without interrupting.

As you listen, don't prejudge. Wait until you've heard all the speaker's ideas before you make a final evaluation. While the speaker is talking, focus your full attention on what is being said. Don't tune out the speaker as you frame your own response. When it's time for you to speak, you can take a moment to collect your thoughts. There's nothing wrong with an interlude of silence.

DON'T BE PRESUMPTUOUS

Good listeners don't presume that they know what the speaker is going to say. But they do try to anticipate the direction of the speaker's thinking. They ask themselves, "Where is this line of reasoning going?" and they follow the speaker through the thinking process.

Questions should be used to help the speaker provide the information you want. They should not be used to grill or cross-examine. Keep your questions brief and open-ended.

Good listeners provide the speaker with feedback. An occasional nod, an "unh huh," and an "I see," tell the speaker that you're still paying attention. When it's your turn to speak, paraphrase the speaker's message as you understand it. This gives the speaker a chance to correct any misinterpretation.

Taking notes is a good sign that you're interested in what you're hearing—unless, of course, the speaker is sharing confidential information intended to be kept private.

"He listens well who takes notes," wrote the Italian poet, Dante, more than 670 years ago. Indeed, the palest ink is better than the most remarkable memory.

Over the years, I've watched how people take notes in my seminars. Some write down everything. Others pick and choose, based on their needs.

Note-taking is an art. If you try to transcribe the whole conversation, you'll be so engrossed in note-taking that you won't have time to absorb, interpret and evaluate the ideas. Just jot down the key points as you listen. The important question is "How will I use this information later, and how easily can I retrieve it?"

WHY PEOPLE DON'T LISTEN

All of us have experienced occasions when we wished we had listened more closely to what was being said. Usually, good listening requires self-discipline, and sometimes it requires self-examination. If you sometimes have problems listening to what others say, some of these factors may be behind the difficulty:

♦ *Prejudice.* You may conclude—either before or during the speaker's remarks—that the speaker has nothing significant to say. The reasons for such prejudice are many. They may include the speaker's appearance, age, actions, voice, race, religion and nationality. All of us carry around petty biases. It's easy to say that we should get rid of them, but prejudices are emotional, not rational, and they can be insidious. It's best to overcome our prejudices, but while we're *overcoming* them we must learn to *override* them when our best interests are involved. You do this by taking charge of your thoughts. Force yourself to seek out the value in what is being said. When you're lost and asking for directions, you don't let your attention stray because the person giving directions is wearing overalls instead of a business suit. You listen for the information you need to get to your destination. When you're inclined to tune out a speaker because of some prejudice, remind yourself of the purpose of the conversation. Keep that purpose in mind, and listen for the words that bear on that purpose.

I once was the victim of such prejudice without knowing it. It wasn't anything I said or did, and it had nothing to do with who I was. It was something my host had said. I was at a Colorado resort, speaking to a group from a Japanese company, and I was the only outside speaker. It was Saturday evening, and my speech was the last event of a program that had begun Monday morning.

I was giving it my best, and I thought I was doing a good job. But something wasn't clicking. The audience wasn't showing the high level of enthusiasm I had expected. Later, I found out why. These people were tired after a grueling week of meetings, and many of them would have preferred to be somewhere else. But their boss had told them that afternoon that they were to hear a professional consultant that evening and that they were to give him the courtesy of listening to him. The boss's remarks made them angry, and built up a prejudice against the "outside consultant." As a result, many of them just sat in self-imposed boredom without bothering to listen to what I had to say.

♦ *Jumping to conclusions.* You may decide that what the speaker is saying is too difficult, too trite, too boring, or otherwise unsuited to your needs. Therefore, you feign attentiveness while your mind is elsewhere. When you encounter this situation, bring your mind back to the here and now. Accept the challenge of drawing from the speaker some ideas and information that will be valuable to you personally. If the message is too trite or too boring, use questions to probe for more interesting and stimulating material. If the information is too difficult, ask the speaker to simplify. Just say, "You're a pro at this, and I'm not. Give it to me in layman's terms." Then don't be afraid to ask questions for clarification. The speaker will be flattered by your interest and will be eager to help you understand.

♦ *Assumption.* You may assume that you already know what the speaker is going to say, so your attention drifts elsewhere. As a result, you miss any new information the speaker may give. When you find yourself thinking this way, make it a game to look for something new to take away from the conversation.

♦ *Inattention.* If you're like most people, you speak about 125 words per minute, but you can think at more than 400 words per minute. As a result, you may use the "spare time" to think of what you're going to say next. In the process, you may miss out on much of what the speaker is saying. The remedy is to use the "spare" time to evaluate and interpret what the speaker is saying. You can frame your own response when it comes your turn to speak.

♦ *Selective listening.* You may sometimes hear only what you want to hear. Once again, the solution is to evaluate and interpret. Look for information and ideas that challenge your own ideas. Compare them with what you know and what you feel. Think about how you might deal with this information or these ideas. Should you reconsider your own position? Should you devise new strategies in light of the information?

♦ *Excessive talking.* If you insist on monopolizing the conversation, you're not going to hear very much. Be conscious of the amount of time you spend talking, and be alert for signs that your listener has something to say. Be willing to yield the floor at reasonable intervals.

♦ *Lack of empathy.* Good listeners try to see things from the speaker's perspective. If you listen strictly from your own perspective, you may miss out on the relevance of what is being said. The speaker's vantage point is an important part of the message.

♦ *Fear.* When you suspect that what is about to be said will reflect unfavorably upon you, fear may result. Many people will stop listening then and find ways to start arguments, or use some other means of escape. Patrick Henry, the fiery patriot of the American Revolution, had the right idea: ". . . Whatever anguish of spirit it may cost, I am willing to know the whole truth; to know the worst, and to provide for it."

Rate yourself as a listener by taking the Listener Quality Quiz in Figure 9–2.

HOW GOOD IS YOUR LQ?

You can test yourself as a listener by taking this Listener Quality Quiz. In the blanks at the end of each listening quality, score yourself on a scale of 1 to 5, with five as a high rating and 1 as a low rating.

1. I always try to give every person I talk with as much time to talk as I take. (____)

2. I really enjoy hearing what other people have to say. (____)

3. I never find it hard to wait until someone else finishes talking before I have my say. (____)

4. I listen, even when I don't particularly like the person who's talking. (____)

5. The sex and age of a person makes no difference in how well I listen. (____)

6. I assume every person has something worthwhile to say and listen intently to friends, acquaintances, and strangers alike. (____)

7. I put away what I am doing while someone is talking. (____)

8. I always look directly at the person who is talking and give that person my full attention, no matter what is on my mind. (____)

9. I encourage others to talk by giving them verbal feedback and asking questions. (____)

10. I encourage other people to talk by my non-verbal messages, such as gestures, facial expressions and posture. (____)

11. I ask for clarification of words and ideas I don't understand. (____)

Figure 9–2

(Continued on the following page)

12. I am sensitive to the tone of the speaker's voice, expressions and gestures that convey meaning. (____)

13. I never interrupt a person who is talking. (____)

14. I withhold all judgments and opinions about what a person is saying until I have heard it all. (____)

15. I listen past the words to the feelings and meanings the person is expressing, and test to see whether I am understanding correctly. (____)

16. I make mental outlines of the main points of what a person is saying. (____)

17. I look mainly for points on which we can agree, not mainly for points on which we disagree. (____)

18. I respect all people's rights to their opinions, even if I disagree with them. (____)

19. I view every dispute or conflict as an opportunity to understand the person better. (____)

20. I recognize that listening is a skill, and I concentrate on trying to develop that skill in my daily life. (____)

Figure 9–2

Scoring: Add up your total points and figure your LQ as follows:
90–100—You're all ears.
80–89—You're a pretty good listener.
70–79—You're missing a lot.
Below 70—You need to follow Shakespeare's advice: "Give every man thy ear but few thy voice."

Once you've mastered the basics of sending and receiving written, spoken and non-verbal messages, you're ready to start applying these skills in specific areas of your life.

Starting with Chapter Ten, we'll cover one of the most sensitive areas of human interaction: communciation between the sexes.

chapter 10

Avoiding the Gender Trap

During the latter half of the 20th century, women entered the American work force in strength. Rosie the Riveter, who moved into the vacant shoes of the men who shipped off to fight World War II, spearheaded the movement of women into the work place. After the war, women refused to go back to the kitchen. They stayed, they called for reinforcements, and they insisted on equal rights. Slowly, but surely, they have won those rights and have justified their place in the work force.

This means that more and more business communications are directed toward women and more and more of them originate with women. If differences exist between the way women communicate and the way men communicate, people of both sexes can increase their effectiveness by learning about these differences. If sexism has permeated the language we speak, it's important that we clear it out and render our communication gender-neutral. This calls for several adjustments in traditional patterns of communication. Three, in particular, stand out.

First, there's the language. The English language had its origins in a male-dominant society, so the concept of male superiority is embedded in the language. This has to change.

Second, because women and men have filled different cultural roles throughout human history, they have developed different manners of communicating. Each has its strengths and drawbacks.

Third, when men and women began working side by side, the issue of sexual harassment entered the work place.

So the advances of women in the business world—in numbers and in stature—pose these communications challenges:

♦ Using the language in a graceful and grammatical, but gender-neutral way.
♦ Learning to understand the communicating style of the opposite sex and to use it yourself when appropriate.
♦ Developing guidelines for interaction that allow conscientious men and women to work comfortably with one other without worrying about the issue of sexual harassment.

THE LANGUAGE CHALLENGE

Some language students infer that the Anglo-Saxon progenitors of our language assumed that men were the norm for the human race and women made up a subcategory. Hence, when the language referred to people in general, it used masculine terms. When it referred to women in particular, it used feminine terms.

We encounter gender problems most often when we are dealing with personal pronouns. For those who put away their English textbooks a long time ago, let me explain what I mean.

We have three sets of pronouns that refer to people:

1. The first-person pronoun refers to the speaker or writer. First-person singular pronouns are *I, me, my* and *mine.* First-person plural pronouns are *we, us, our* and *ours.*
2. Second-person pronouns refer to the person to whom the communication is addressed. They are the same in both singular and plural form. They are *you, your* and *yours.*
3. Third-person pronouns refer to third parties. Third-person singular pronouns are *he, she, it, him, her, his, her, hers* and *its.* Third-person plural pronouns are *they, them, their* and *theirs.*

Notice that only one set of pronouns—the third person singular—makes a distinction between males and females. The rest of the pronouns are gender neutral—that is, they can apply equally to either sex or to both sexes.

The problem arises when we need a singular pronoun that can refer to either or both sexes. The only third-person singular pronouns we have that are gender neutral are *it* and *its,* and we usually use those words to refer only to animals or inanimate objects.

The traditional answer to this dilemma has been to use the masculine pronoun to represent either or both sexes.

ABE THE SEXIST?

To illustrate the problem—and to dramatize the way times have changed—let's look at a highly sexist statement by a man whose name is still synonymous with equality and justice: Abraham Lincoln. Lincoln once made this observation:

> *It is difficult to make a man miserable while he feels he is worthy of himself and claims kindred to the great God who made him.*

Any politician who uttered those words today would be greeted with cries of outrage: "What about women? Aren't they, too, kindred to the great God who made them?"

Some people would have edited the statement to read:

> *It is difficult to make a person miserable while she or he feels he or she is worthy of herself or himself and claims kindred to the great God who made him or her.*

Abe would have been caught in a bind. On the one hand, his statement would have satisfied the requirements of gender neutrality by using both masculine and feminine pronouns and by alternating them so that half the time the feminine pronoun came first and half the time the masculine pronoun came first. It also would have met the grammatical requirements. But the statement would have been hopelessly awkward and worthless as a literary effort.

GENDER-NEUTRAL PRONOUNS

What does one do?

At the turn of the 21st century, there are two alternatives. One is to draft plural pronouns for double duty as singular pronouns when you refer to either or both genders.

Following this procedure, Lincoln would have said:

> *It is difficult to make a person miserable while they feel they are worthy of themselves and claim kindred to the great God who made them.*

In this case, Abe would be letting the plural pronouns *they, themselves* and *them* stand in for the singular *person.* That's what most people do in everyday conversation, but the usage still sets the grammatical purist's teeth on edge.

It can be argued that it is far more logical to use a plural pronoun to stand in for a single person than to use a masculine pronoun to stand in for a feminine person. This logic is likely to prevail in the 21st century, and it's my prediction that by the end of the first decade of the new millennium *they, them, their* and *theirs* will be perfectly acceptable as singular neuter pronouns. The question of whether we'll use *themselves* or *themself* is up in the air, but I'm betting on *themselves.*

In the meantime, if you want to be gender neutral and avoid the awkwardness of *he/she* and *him/her* while remaining perfectly grammatical, there is a way. As we've seen, any plural pronoun can refer to either or both genders. So can any pronoun in the first or second-person.

Therefore, you can usually solve the gender dilemma by switching to the plural or to the first or second person.

Abe could have reworded his remarks this way:

> *It is difficult to make people miserable while they feel they are worthy of themselves and claim kindred to the great God who made them.*

Or, if he preferred, he could have switched to the first person:

> *It is difficult to make us miserable while we feel we are worthy of ourselves and claim kindred to the great God who made us.*

Or he could have followed the common—and grammatical—practice of using the second-person pronoun to refer to people in general:

> *It is difficult to make you miserable while you feel you are worthy of yourself and claim kindred to the great God who made you.*

Most situations that call for gender-neutral pronouns can be handled through one or another of these devices. So if you're running a restaurant, you can post a sign saying "All who handle food must wash their hands after using the bathroom," or "If you handle food, you must wash your hands after using the bathroom." But if the sign says "Everyone who handles food must wash their hands after using the bathroom," the Health Department won't complain; nor will the servers and customers, unless they happen to be English teachers or fussy writers.

RAISING CONSCIOUSNESS

The other problems of gender neutrality are relatively easy to fix. They usually call for nothing more than consciousness raising.

Here are some areas for attention:

♦ *Find substitutes for compound nouns that contain "man" or "woman" as part of the word.*

A common strategy is to substitute *person* for *man* or *woman.* If you choose this strategy, be sure that you don't use *person* only when referring to women or to people of both genders. If you refer to a woman as a *spokesperson* while you refer to a man as a *spokesman,* you're still being sexist.

Figure 10–1 shows some examples of sexist words and their gender-neutral equivalents.

The same rule applies to such words as *forefathers* and the expression *city fathers.* I hate to pick on Honest Abe, but when he stated that "Our forefathers brought forth on this continent a new nation . . . ," he ignored half the population of the American colonies.

SEXIST	GENDER NEUTRAL
Spokesman	Spokesperson, Representative
Policeman	Police officer
Fireman	Firefighter
Congressman	Representative, Member of Congress
Chairman	Chairperson, Chair
Postman	Mail carrier
Repairman	Repairer
Workman	Worker
Craftsman	Artisan
Alderman	Board member
Salesman	Salesperson
Businessman	Businessperson

Figure 10–1

"Ancestors" and "forebears" are terms that embrace both forefathers and foremothers. *City leaders* is a gender-neutral way of describing the mayor and governing body of a municipality.

♦ *Avoid other words that tend to stereotype male/female roles.*

For some reason, English-users have a hang-up about using words ending in -er and -or to refer to women—even though the suffixes were originally applied to women. When the word describes an occupational function or role, we seem compelled to add an -ess, an -ette or a -trix to the root word. What difference does it make whether the aircraft is flown by an *aviator* or an *aviatrix,* so long as it takes off and lands safely? Can you look at a statue and tell whether its creator was a sculptor or a sculptress? Does a steak served by a *waiter* taste different from one served by a *waitress?* Do authors punch the keyboard differently from *authoresses?* (Fortunately, we don't have to refer to a woman radio or television journalist as a *broadcastress.*)

When recruiting personnel, in particular, businesses should be careful to use gender-neutral terms. Usually, there's a handy non-sexist term that serves very well in place of the sexist term. If you balk at calling both men and women *aviators,* call them pilots. Most restaurants now call the people who bring your food *servers.* Patricia Aburdene and John Naisbitt are both authors. They're also *writers* (nobody ever refers to a *writress.*)

♦ *When referring to both sexes, alternate between mentioning males first and females first.*

Sometimes, even when they're making an obvious effort to be gender neutral, people show a bias toward the masculine. This applies to female as well as male communicators. When we're trying to avoid using the masculine pronoun to refer to either sex, we almost invariably substitute *he or she.* We refer to *men and women, husbands and wives,* and *boys and girls.* The expressions *bride and groom* and *ladies and gentlemen* are exceptions. In common practice, we place the masculine term first. To be gender neutral, alternate the terms.

♦ *When using stories and illustrations, use female as well as male examples.*

The female has been slighted in literature and folklore, and so we have fallen into the habit of slighting her in our portrayal of workplace situations. I learned this lesson first-hand while speaking at a management conference for AT&T in New Jersey a few years ago. The audience consisted of men and women. During the break, a woman executive reminded me that all my examples were masculine-oriented. Since then, I've included feminine and masculine examples in my repertoire of yarns. And I try to avoid sexist stereotypes. I don't automatically assume that an executive or manager is a *he* and a stenographer or bookkeeper is a *she.*

♦ *Remember that women are adults.*

Modern women often resent it when men refer to them as *girls.* The male executive who says "I'll have my girl type up the report" is being blatantly sexist. "Secretary" is a perfectly good term, and it's gender-neutral: We call the head of the federal Commerce Department the secretary of commerce, regardless of whether the post is filled by a man or a woman. The male boss who casually invites "the girls and guys at the office" to a cookout at his home may get by with it. But it's always safer to say "women and men" or "the whole gang."

Men often show distinctions by referring to men by last names and women by first names. If an executive says, "Johnson, I want you and Pat to collaborate on that project," you can bet that Johnson is a man and Pat is a woman. If you refer to men by last names only, refer to women the same way. Personally, I prefer the more casual first-name approach in work-place situations and other informal settings, and the use of courtesy titles on more formal occasions. All my friends, associates and employees—including my secretaries—call me Nido when we're interacting at work, and I call them by their first names.

THE WAY MEN AND WOMEN COMMUNICATE

Men and women have traditionally communicated in different ways. This has led to misunderstandings, both in the work place and in the home. Even today, the legacy of cultural conditioning can be detected in the communication habits of men and women. Members of both sexes should be aware of the differences and learn to take them into account.

We could easily fall into the trap of stereotyping masculine and feminine communication styles, and that would be unfair to both sexes. Men are often stereotyped as the forceful communicators, though I've known women on all continents who speak as forcefully as any man without sacrificing their femininity. Women are often assumed to be more nurturing and caring in their choice of language, but I've known men who are secure in their masculinity, yet speak as gently as any woman. As time goes by, I suspect that men and women will become more alike in the way they express themselves. I don't think this will be a case of women learning to talk like men. I expect to see men and women emulate the best in both styles of communication so that we finally arrive at a truly gender-neutral style of communicating.

WHO SAID IT?

To illustrate the characteristics traditionally associated with male and female language, read these quotations and see which sex they suggest:

♦ *Dammit! I broke my fingernail.*
• *Oh dear! I just broke my nail!*

♦ *That's a nice-looking little statue on your bookcase.*
• *That's an adorable figurine on your bookcase.*

♦ *You'll have to go back and refigure that bid.*
• *Shouldn't you go back and refigure that bid?*

♦ *Fifty percent is too big a mark-up for that product.*
• *A fifty-percent mark-up is a bit high for that product, don't you think?*

Most people would identify the first statement in each pair as masculine in tone and the second as feminine, even though a man or a woman might have uttered any of them without sacrificing sexual identity.

Casey Miller and Kate Swift—two women who studied the language habits of males and females—characterize the differences between male and female communications this way:

> *Males adopt a more direct, forceful way of talking; females a more tentative, questioning approach. What one typically phrases as a statement or command the other formulates as a request.*[1]

University of California linguist Robin Lakoff attributes this to cultural conditioning:

> *Discouraged from expressing herself forcefully, a girl may acquire speech habits that communicate uncertainty, hesitancy, indecisiveness and subordination."*[2]

DIFFERENT EXPLETIVES AND ADJECTIVES

Other students of male/female conversation maintain that women traditionally have used different expletives from men. They are more likely to shun profanity and to favor polite language. Men are more likely than women to use **Damn! Son of a gun! Holy mackerel! Great Caesar!** and **By thunder!** along with other, more explicit expressions. Women are more likely to say **Darn! Oh dear! Mercy! For goodness sake!** and **Good heavens!**

But these are broad generalizations. Some women are capable of salty speech, too, and some men shun even the mildest profanity.

Women traditionally have used adjectives that reflect deeper feelings than the ones men use. What's **good-looking** to a man will be **lovely** to a woman. What's **nice** to a man will be **adorable** to a woman. What's **great** to a man will be **wonderful** to a woman.

That doesn't mean that a man who thinks a rose is **lovely** is somehow effeminate or that a woman who says **holy mackerel** is being "mannish." It's just that one sex has historically shown a preference for one type of adjective and expletive while another sex has preferred another type.

Women shouldn't worry about using the terms that come natural to them, regardless of which sex they're associated with. And neither should men.

WHEN A QUESTION BECOMES A STATEMENT

But notice two other sentences in that group. The statement, "You'll have to go back and refigure that bid," is associated with masculine communication, while the question, "Shouldn't you go back and refigure that bid?" is associated with femininity. The assertive statement, "Fifty percent is too big a mark-up for that product," is assumed to come from a man, while the tentative statement, "A fifty-percent mark-up is a bit high for that product, don't you think?" is assumed to be from a woman.

According to students of male/female communication differences, the man is more likely to put his communication in the form of an assertive directive. Many women (and some men) prefer to put it in the form of a tentative question.

Women, says Lakoff, are more likely to use the "tag question" such as "don't you think?" at the end of their opinions. Even when she doesn't conclude with a question, a woman may raise her voice at the end of the sentence so that "Meet you at 7?" becomes a question rather than a statement.

"By seeming to leave decisions open and not imposing a viewpoint on others, women's language comes off sounding more polite than men's," she observed.[3]

Deborah Tannen, Ph.D., linguistics professor at Georgetown University in Washington, D.C., did extensive research into the way men and women communicate. She maintains that men usually grow up in a world based on a hierarchical social order. In their world, she says, "conversations are negotiations in which people try to achieve and maintain the upper hand if they can, and protect themselves from others' attempts to put them down and push them around. Life, then is a contest, a struggle to preserve independence and avoid failure."

A woman, however, approaches the world "as an individual in a network of connections. In this world, conversations are negotiations for closeness in which people try to seek and give confirmation and support, and to reach consensus. They try to protect themselves from others' attempts to push them away. Life, then, is a community, a struggle to preserve intimacy and avoid isolation. Though there are hierarchies in this world too, they are hierarchies more of friendship than of power and accomplishment."[4]

We don't have to agree with Tannen's conclusions about the motives behind the different styles of communicating. It's enough to recognize that differences do exist, and that some of the differences correlate to a greater or lesser degree with differences between the sexes. The differences do not mark one style of communication as superior and another style as inferior. All they tell us is that when an executive says "A 50% mark-up is a bit high for the product, don't you think?" she is not necessarily asking your opinion. She is probably making a statement in a style traditionally associated with women.

Tannen likened conversation between the sexes to cross-cultural communication. Even body language is different, she found. Women tend to align themselves face to face and maintain eye contact, but men and boys tend to sit at an angle, or even parallel to each other, and look around, glancing at each other occasionally. To a man, a woman's direct gaze may be taken as flirtatious while a man's direct gaze may be taken as challenging.[5]

Lakoff maintained that the purpose of women's "special language" was to "submerge a woman's personal identity. Discouraged from expressing herself forcefully, a girl may acquire speech habits that communicate uncertainty, hesitancy, indecisiveness and subordination."[6]

Tannen attributes the differences to the woman's search for intimacy as opposed to the man's search for independence. Because of these differences, she says, a woman is likely to listen politely to conversation that doesn't particularly interest her, while a man is more likely to try to take control of the conversation rather than allow the other person to get the upper hand.

"What is the hope for the future?" she asks. "Must we play out our assigned parts to the closing act?"

Her answer:

Although we tend to fall back on habitual ways of talking, repeating old refrains and familiar lines, habits can be broken. Women and men both can gain by understanding the other gender's style and by learning to use it on occasion.

Women who find themselves unwillingly cast as the listener should practice propelling themselves out of that position rather than waiting patiently for the lecture to end. Perhaps they need to give up the belief that they must wait for the floor to be handed to them. If they have something to say on a subject, they might push themselves to volunteer it. If they are bored with a subject, they can exercise some influence on the conversation and change the topic to something they would rather discuss.[7]

WOMEN DON'T HAVE TO SOUND LIKE MEN

Women don't have to sound like men to be forceful and assertive. But they do need to be aware of the way men might perceive some of their communication characteristics.

This awareness can be invaluable in the marketplace when women are trying to sell to men or to buy from them. It can also be highly useful for women corporate leaders who must manage or supervise men and who must deal with male peers on the management team.

What a woman perceives as politeness, a man might interpret as indecisiveness, and reluctance to make a commitment. The 21st century woman needs to cultivate assertiveness, just as the male with the macho self-image needs to cultivate tact. There's a good middle ground that will serve both sexes well.

Women need not sound like "one of the boys" to convey self-confidence and poise in a business setting. They need only speak as if they believe firmly in what they're saying. When they give instructions, they can phrase them tactfully, but give them in a confident voice, as if they expect them to be carried out.

THE STRONG FEMALE VOICE

A woman's voice is different from a man's voice, and there's no need for women to try to change. The late 20th century brought a healthy crop of successful women broadcasters to the television news shows. Network stars such as Barbara Walters, Diane Sawyer and Connie Chung demonstrated that the female voice could speak with authority. Remember Barbara Jordan, who held the 1976 Democratic National Convention spellbound and went on to become a federal judge? Dallas columnist Molly Ivins wrote, tongue-in-cheek, of her fellow Texan that she "can't help sounding like God Almighty."[7] Yet Jordan spoke in a rich, feminine voice. Ann Richards, who went on to become governor of Texas, keynoted the 1988 Democratic National Convention in a decidedly feminine voice. Elizabeth Dole, George Bush's secretary of labor, spoke effectively and authoritatively in her soft North Carolina accent. There was nothing weak or tentative in the communication styles of any of these women.

The point is: Whether you're a man or a woman, a strong, low-pitched voice conveys calmness, confidence and authority. Your lower voice range is your best for assertive communication. A higher pitch signals excitement, and sometimes nervousness and fear.

SEXUAL HARASSMENT

When women began filling positions formerly reserved for men, some men clung stubbornly to the asinine notion that women were created for the gratification of men and were therefore fair game for sexual advances. Some women still clung to the notion that their femininity was an asset to be exploited, and were willing to use it to gain work-place advantages.

Sexual harassment became a work-place issue. When Anita Hill, an Oklahoma professor, accused Supreme Court nominee Clarence Thomas of sexual harassment while she was working with him, the harassment issue was dramatized on the American national stage. Everybody talked about it.

Both men and women began to wonder where the line was to be drawn between friendly patter and sexual communication. Women became more ready to draw the line, and even some men began to come forward to complain about harassment from female bosses and associates.

IMAGINE YOUR SPOUSE IS THERE

A simple rule should suffice in governing behavior between the sexes in the work place: Always conduct yourself as you would if your spouse or the other person's spouse were in the room with you.

Even if neither you nor your co-worker of the opposite sex is married or committed to someone else, conduct yourself as if both of you were. This applies particularly when you're dealing with people under your supervision.

People vary in their acceptance of sexual patter. Some enjoy it. Some are embarrassed and even intimidated by it. Be safe—and considerate. Avoid off-color jokes and sexually suggestive remarks. Don't flirt on the job and never suggest—even in jest—that sexual favors might lead to more favorable treatment on the job while sexual indifference might hold back advancement.

Every business should draw up a policy on sexual harassment. Both men and women should play a role in drafting it. It should set clear guidelines for what behavior is acceptable and what is unacceptable. It should provide a specific procedure for reporting and resolving harassment charges. It should also provide specific penalties, and those penalties should be enforced.

ETIQUETTE BETWEEN THE SEXES

Attitudes are communicated through the little courtesies we show to other people, but in the changing world of gender relations, little courtesies can be misinterpreted. Actions that once communicated a sense of courtesy and a concern for proper etiquette may now be regarded as signs of condescending and patronizing attitudes.

Should a man open doors for women? Should men light women's cigarettes? Should men and women shake hands with each other in social situations?

The rule of thumb: If you normally provide a courtesy for a person of the same sex, provide the same courtesy for a person of the opposite sex. Don't expect a member of the opposite sex to do things for you that you wouldn't expect a member of your own sex to do.

In business settings, women want to be and expect to be treated as fully equal to men. If you're walking side by side with a client or business associate and you reach the door first, it's common courtesy to open the door and hold it for the other person—regardless of gender.

Most women no longer expect male business associates or clients to get out of the car, walk around and open the door for them. And it's no longer mandatory, in a business setting, for a man to light a cigarette for a woman. In social settings, the rules vary according to the individuals involved.

The presence of women has enriched the work place, greatly enlarged the pool of talent, and increased the level of justice and equity in our country. The company that takes full advantage of the talents of both sexes doubles its prospects for success. And the individuals who learn to communicate effectively across gender lines in gender-neutral fashion are powerfully positioned to share in that success.

The gender factor, though, is not the only element of diversity in the modern work place. The American population is becoming a kaleidoscope of cultures, and this variety is being reflected in the work place. The European work place is also becoming more diverse as people from North Africa, Asia and other former colonial areas look for opportunities on the Continent, and as southern Europeans go job-hunting in the industrialized north. In the next chapter we will explore avenues of cross-cultural communication in the work place.

Cross-Cultural Communication

Those who lead the American work force of the 21st century must learn to communicate with a variety of cultures. The work force has changed because American demographics have changed. The monochrome, predominantly male environment of the early 20th century is gone, never to return. In its place is a colorful demographic brocade, drawing together people from nations and cultures around the globe. Out of this ethnic and cultural mixture will be drawn the leaders of tomorrow. Today's leadership must find ways to bring the non-white and the non-male employee into the circles of leadership. It is not just a matter of fairness; it is a matter of necessity.

THE DWINDLING WORK FORCE

Because of the baby bust that followed the baby boom, the growth in the work force is dwindling. In 1980, there were 41 million Americans in their 20s. The twenty-something population for the year 2000 is projected at 34 million. The *Training and Development Journal* projects that between now and 2020, the size of the working-age population will increase by less than 1% a year.[1] The growth rate for the working-age minority populations will be much higher; the growth rate for non-Hispanic white males will be somewhat lower. If the economy grows by about 2% a year, business can expect a growing deficit in the labor pool. There won't be enough white men to fill the ranks. This means that, even without Equal Employment Opportunity legislation, and setting aside all considerations of fairness and ethics, businesses will have to hire, develop and promote women and minorities. In the 21st century, women and minorities will constitute the great majority of the work force.

Even in the mid-nineties, white men made up only 44% of the work force, while they constituted less than 40% of the total population. By the year 2000, their percentage of the working population will have shrunk significantly because of immigration and higher birth rates among minorities. In addition, a new generation of women will have grown up in the ranks of business, eager for the challenges of leadership and unwilling to be relegated to subordinate roles.

The American heritage is no longer a European but a global heritage. At the outset of the '90s, our population included 30 million African-Americans. If they occupied a separate country, it would have more people than 48 of the 52 African countries. The 22.4 million Hispanics in the United States outnumber the total population of all but three of the Spanish-speaking countries of Latin America.

The 7.3 million Americans of Asian or Pacific-island descent outnumber the populations of more than half the countries in Asia and the Pacific. You'll see more Oriental faces in America than you will see in Cambodia, Laos, Hong Kong or Singapore.

Within our boundaries are about two million American Indians—close to the population of Panama.

What's more, their numbers are growing. As the chart in Figure 11-1 shows, the Asian/Pacific population of the United States nearly doubled between 1980 and 1990. The Hispanic population grew by more than 50%, while the African-American population expanded by 13.2%. Meanwhile, the population of non-Hispanic whites grew by 5%.

Non-Hispanic whites still constitute the majority of the American population, but at some point during the 21st century, this will change. Non-Hispanic whites will simply be the largest of several minorities in the nation and in the work place.

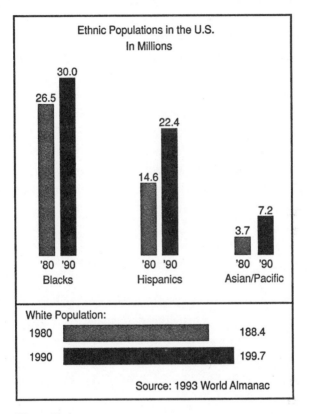

Figure 11–1

This means that corporate leaders, from CEOs to supervisors, must learn to deal with and motivate a work force that springs from a variety of different cultures. They must also learn to do business in the global marketplace, which demands a knowledge of and sensitivity to the ways of other cultures.

LANGUAGE INSTRUCTION

In many cases, companies have found it advantageous to offer their employees courses in English as a second language. California Literacy, organized to provide literacy training through community colleges in its state, emphasized English as a second language. Its approach was to use manuals, training materials and other written materials taken from the work place itself.

The Honeywell Corporation carried its language instruction one step further. It discovered that Minneapolis, the site of its headquarters, had the second largest concentration of Southeast Asians in the United States. Many of these Asians were finding jobs at Honeywell, and the language barrier was becoming a problem. Honeywell not only provided English-language courses for the Vietnamese, Laotians and Cambodians in its work force; it also provided instruction in Asian languages for its American-born personnel.

FEELING AT HOME WITH DIVERSITY

If you want to obtain top performance from your work force, you can't afford to have a substantial percentage of employees feeling like outsiders. Businesses must look for ways to make people from diverse backgrounds feel comfortable while working with one another. This means providing environments in which people will be respected regardless of gender, skin color, language background or national origin.

Honeywell began with awareness training for its personnel. It looked for similarities rather than differences, and focused on cultivating attitudes of respect. Then it provided more skill-based education, teaching the techniques for managing a diverse work force.

Too often, people tend to look at other ethnic and cultural groups through stereotypical lenses. All races and cultures have been affected by the forces of history, but we also share common human characteristics. The more we get to know one another, the more we recognize the similarities and the more we see people as individual humans instead of members of some special group. We come to recognize the absurdity of stereotyping and the dangers it entails.

The best way to understand people from another culture is to establish lines of communication. You'll learn a lot more by asking than you will by observing. One way to ask people about themselves is to organize special-interest groups for ethnics within the work force. Then meet with them and let them tell you about their problems and concerns.

FIND OUT WHAT OFFENDS

It's up to the company to create an environment that is congenial to all racial, ethnic and national groups. That environment is nourished through countless day-to-day interactions between management and employees and among peers.

These interactions will be more harmonious if we understand that communications are sent and received through cultural filters. I've had to adjust my cultural lenses repeatedly as my consulting work has taken me to the Middle East, the Pacific Rim, Australia and New Zealand, and across Europe.

I've learned that words, expressions and gestures that mean one thing in your culture may mean something else in another culture. A term that may seem perfectly harmless to you may be offensive to someone from another ethnic group. A gesture that may be offensive to you may be a friendly communication to someone from another culture.

People who deal with persons from other cultures, including those who supervise them, should be sensitive to the attitudes that go along with the culture.

How can we know what to do and say when dealing with people of other ethnic and cultural groups?

First, find out what terms and expressions are offensive to the ears of others. Never use derogatory terms to describe people of racial, ethnic or national minorities, even in joking.

Sometimes it may be difficult to find out what is or is not offensive to minorities. The word Negro was once perfectly acceptable to Americans of African descent, since it is derived from a Latin word meaning "black." "Colored people" was a euphemism that became enshrined in the name of one of the most active and effective organizations for African-Americans: the National Association for the Advancement of Colored People (NAACP). But today, those terms are considered passe at best and patronizing and insulting at worst. The corrupted, slovenly pronunciation of Negro is deeply offensive to most American blacks. During the civil-rights revolution, "black" became the preferred descriptive, and "African-American" gained acceptance during the '80s and '90s.

'WE PEOPLE' VS. 'YOU PEOPLE'

But don't be patronizing. Many white Americans wear their racial tolerance on their sleeves and go out of their way to demonstrate that they're not bigots. Black Americans have fought long and hard for equal treatment in the work place and in society at large. Most of them don't want special treatment. They want to be treated as Americans and not as black Americans. While they may take great pride in their cultural roots, they still regard themselves as a part of the American fabric—as indeed they are.

When presidential candidate Ross Perot addressed a black audience as "you people" in 1992, he lost points, even though he was trying to assure them that he was in sympathy with their aspirations. The preamble to the American Constitution begins with the words "We, the people of the United States of America." Today, "We, the people" embraces citizens of all races, cultures and national origins. There should be no such thing as "you people" when addressing fellow members of the corporate family. If you can't say "we people," you need to brush up on your intercultural communication.

WHAT IS A NAVAJO?

No one has developed a completely satisfying name for the people who were inhabiting the Americas when Columbus arrived.

148

Columbus called them "Indians" because he thought he had found the Indies of the Orient. If you use that name, you have to be sure to distinguish the American Indian from natives of India. "Native American" is a recent terminology, but what does that make people of European, African or Asian descent who were born in the USA?

When the Europeans first came to America, the native inhabitants didn't perceive themselves as one people. They perceived themselves as Algonquins, Iroquois, Cherokee, Apache, Dakota, Navajo and Aztecs. It's quite acceptable to refer to people by tribal name, but if you have to use an all-encompassing name, listen to the individual's conversation and be guided by the preference you observe. Or just ask.

BEWARE ETHNIC SLANG

Some words that may be considered innocent by native-born white Americans may be offensive to minorities. Most Asians don't want to be called "Asiatics," because the term harks back to the days of colonialism.

"Chinaman" and "Jap" are unacceptable in any context. So are such derogatory nicknames as "Gook," "Chink," "Wop," "Mick," "Paddy," "Span," "Dago," "Hymie," and "Hebe." These words should be entirely banished from the vocabularies of 21st century leaders.

ENGLISH IS PRECISE BUT BLUNT

English is a precise language, but it is perceived as blunt by many speakers of other languages.

Americans often pride themselves on "straight talk" and "telling it like it is." This is a turn-off to Japanese workers, who practice "ishin-denshin"—communication by the heart. To the Japanese, the truth lies in the things you imply, and is not openly stated. Vagueness is preferred to precision. If you're too explicit with the Japanese, they take that as the mark of a know-it-all.

This highly diplomatic approach is common among Asian cultures. In some languages, diplomacy is taken to such an extreme that there is no word for "no."

Facial expressions can be deceptive, too. The Japanese are taught not to burden other people with their problems. Therefore, the bright smile on a Japanese face may mask a heart full of disappointment or despair.

But the face can often be a more accurate message-carrier than the tongue.

KNOWING WHEN YOU'RE GETTING THROUGH

Suppose you're trying to give Mei Ling, your Chinese accountant, some technical on-the-job instructions.

If you say "Do you understand?" Mei Ling will probably say "Yes," even though she is totally in the dark. Why?

Mei Ling doesn't want to lose face, and she doesn't want you to lose face. If she says "No," it can only mean one of two things to her: She is too dense to comprehend or you are a poor instructor.

In such cases, it's important to watch the face. It's hard to disguise puzzlement, and it's usually easy enough to tell whether the face comprehends.

Be alert for indications that you're not getting through. Ask for feedback. If your listener repeats what you've said exactly in your words, you probably didn't get through. Listen for questions. People who are following your thoughts usually ask pertinent questions to expand their understanding. If there are no questions, there's likely to be no understanding. And be suspicious when you encounter too much nodding agreement. A person who understands what you're saying will usually find something to elaborate on or to disagree about.

USE STANDARD ENGLISH

It didn't take me long, after I came to America, to discover that the English language is full of bewildering idioms. In idioms, words take on meanings that are quite different from their dictionary definitions. For instance, when you say "I give up," you mean "I surrender," "I quit," or "I yield." But the newcomer to the English language may be puzzled. What does it mean to make a gift in an upward direction?

Not long after I came to this country, I went into a drugstore, made a purchase and was on my way to the door.

"Come back," said the cashier, in a friendly North Carolina accent.

I turned and went back to the counter.

"What did you want?" I asked.

"Nothing," she said.

"But you told me to come back."

The people in the store went into hysterics.

In the Southern United States, "Come back" is a friendly parting expression that means, "Come back to see us some time" or, in a commercial setting, "I hope you'll do business with us again."

"How are you?" was another expression I had to get used to. I soon learned that this is seldom an inquiry into your health or circumstances. It's another way of saying "hello," and the only response called for is "Fine, how are you?"

You won't be able to clear all idioms from your speech when you address foreign-born workers on the job; nor should you. Idioms are important tools of communication, and newcomers to English must learn them just as they must learn individual words. But be aware that you may occasionally have to explain carefully what you mean. When you ask, "Can you run this machine?" your listener may think you mean "Can you pick up this machine and run with it?"

Slang or jargon should be avoided until the employee has become fluent in English. Use simple, standard-English expressions and you'll communicate more effectively.

PROVIDE GOOD ORIENTATION

When you're dealing with people from another background, learn as much about them as you can. Go to the encyclopedia or to the card catalog at the library. Find out whether there are ethnic organizations that might provide some information. Ask for help from a member of that ethnic group who has already fully adapted to the American culture. And ask the newcomers themselves: "Ishaq, I know you're going to find things different here from the way they are in Pakistan. I want to be as helpful to you as I can. Please come to me with any questions you have, and let me know if the way we do things conflicts in any way with your customs and beliefs."

Mentoring can also be used as an adjustment tool for immigrants. The ideal mentor would be one who is familiar with both cultures. If such a person is not available, then look for someone with an abundance of friendliness, tolerance and tact. Give mentors good orientations into the other culture and let them know what to expect in the way of behavior or reactions.

You can give employees from other cultures a sense of belonging to the group by seeking their suggestions and comments. The special-interest groups mentioned earlier can provide useful insights. But some people may be reluctant to provide open criticism, even in the non-threatening environment of a focus group. So the wise executive will provide a system whereby employees can make comments and suggestions anonymously. That way, you get the benefit of feedback and nobody loses face.

ADMINISTERING DISCIPLINE

Sometimes members of the majority culture may feel uncomfortable about disciplining someone from an ethnic or cultural minority.

We should certainly be sensitive to the way our words and actions might be perceived. Yet, it is entirely proper to expect people to measure up to reasonable standards of performance and conduct.

Make sure that all employees understand what is expected and know the consequences of failure to measure up. This should be spelled out clearly in written policy. This policy should be explained in clear language upon hiring.

When the standards are not met, the first step should be a courteous and helpful reminder, delivered in private. When sterner measures are required, it's wise to confer with someone who is familiar with the culture and ask for advice. Plan your approach and follow it.

THE LANGUAGE OF CULTURE

While human nature is basically the same no matter what culture you're dealing with, the language of words, gestures and customs— the language of culture—differs widely.

American soldiers in Vietnam often stood casually with hands on hips when talking to each other or to native Vietnamese. This could be unsettling to a Vietnamese. In their culture, standing with hands on hips means that you're very angry and are getting ready to throw a punch.

When Nikita Khrushchev held his hands aloft at the United Nations and seemed to be shaking hands with himself, many Americans interpreted that as boorish behavior. Russians recognized it as a friendly gesture.

If you're introduced to a French person who gives your hand one quick shake, then drops it abruptly, don't be offended. That's the standard handshake in France. If your new French friend clinches his right hand into a fist and jerks his thumb toward his mouth, don't walk away in a huff. You're being invited to have a drink.

If you call to a Japanese worker across a crowded room and she puts her finger to her nose, she is not giving you a gesture of disrespect. She's just asking, "Are you talking to me?" An American would point to the chest, not to the nose.

DIFFERENT PERCEPTIONS

If an American salesperson talks to an English client over lunch, the Briton will probably speak in a low voice that can be heard only by the salesperson. The American's voice will become louder as enthusiasm grows. The Briton doesn't want to intrude on the privacy of others in the restaurant. The American wants to demonstrate sincerity and commitment. What the American perceives as openness, the English person perceives as thoughtlessness. What the Briton perceives as being discreet, the American perceives as being timid.

The Japanese are more like the British. Americans have a saying that "it's the squeaky wheel that gets the grease." The Japanese have a saying, "The pheasant that doesn't cry won't get shot."

Americans are a gregarious people; to them silence is something to be avoided. Dr. Edward T. Hall, professor of anthropology at Illinois Institute of Technology, once told of an American family that was host to an Arab student. The family became upset with their guest at one point and decided to give him the "silent treatment." The cold shoulder went unnoticed. In the Arab culture, you don't have to go off into another room to be alone. You can simply fall silent, and people will grant you your privacy without taking offense. So the young Arab had no way of knowing that his American hosts were upset with him.[2]

INVISIBLE BUBBLES

Different cultures move in "invisible" bubbles of different sizes. The "invisible bubble" refers to the distance we normally keep from other people when we're interacting. You will normally stand closer to an intimate acquaintance than to a stranger.

Latin Americans have small invisible bubbles. They like to move in close and talk animatedly.

On the other hand, hearty back-slapping behavior that might go over well among Americans of European and African descent might embarrass people from Oriental cultures who are accustomed to more formality.

EYE CONTACT

Eye contact is perceived in different ways in different cultures. The English will gaze steadily into the eyes of their conversational partners as a sign of interest and involvement. Americans, having been taught that it's impolite to stare, will look the other person in the eye, but will look away occasionally. The Japanese will look down as a sign of respect.

If you're the supervisor and you stop to make friendly banter with some workers from the Orient, they may suspect that you're checking up on them. In some Eastern cultures, socializing on the job is taboo.

What all this means is that you must be aware of cultural differences when you're dealing with people in the work place and the market place.

CULTURAL PROFILES

If a number of different cultures are represented in your work force, it might be helpful to prepare cultural profiles for each employee from a minority culture. Make this profile a part of the employee's personnel records. The profile might contain information on language, religion, food customs or restrictions, the political system in the homeland, national and religious holidays, and customs that might affect work habits.

This same type of profile can be vital to executives and salespeople who must deal with peers in other cultures.

One reason the Japanese have been so much more successful in the American market than Americans have been in the Japanese market is that the Japanese have studied our culture. They know our language and they know our behavior.

Americans have not yet learned to communicate effectively with the Japanese. We expect our democratic, egalitarian behavior to go over well in other cultures. When two American CEOs sit down to negotiate, with their respective management teams beside them, everybody tries to be comfortable with one another. The CEO's staff may address her by first name, and may even argue with her good-naturedly. In many other cultures—including the Japanese—rank has its privileges, and among them is the respect and deference of those of lower rank.

SELLING ACROSS CULTURES

Sales approaches will differ from culture to culture. Americans like to exchange preliminary pleasantries, then get down to business. To the Japanese, the pleasantries are the heart of the procedure. A deal an American might close within 25 minutes could stretch into hours for the Japanese, for whom a night on the town might be a part of the process.

Americans, of course, are no strangers to the practice of conducting business on the golf course. But whereas an American would try to turn in an impressive performance, the Japanese would take pains to lose the match rather than humiliate the other person.

You cannot learn, in one chapter of one book, everything you need to know about every culture you will encounter in the American work place or the global market place. Nor will I try to make this chapter the single reference source for this subject. It's just a quick reminder that the diverse work force and the global marketplace require a global perspective and a willingness to get to know and understand people from other backgrounds.

All of us must become aware that the American style of communication is not the only style, and that it is possible for people with the best of intentions to be misunderstood in embarrassing and offensive ways when communicating with people of other languages and cultures.

BLENDING THE HYPHENS INTO TWO-LETTER WORDS

When you're dealing with people of other cultures, make a conscious effort to learn as much as you can about the culture. Listen to the people with whom you communicate. Look for ways to obtain feedback. And remember, the ways of other cultures may seem strange to you, but they're normal to the people who practice them. And the ways that are familiar to you may be strange and bewildering to others.

We must understand and accept the fact that all cultures—including our own—have their peculiarities, but that humans in every culture are basically similar. That's why I can conduct seminars in Auckland, New Zealand, Frankfurt, Germany, Montreal, Canada, and Kuala Lumpur, Malaysia—all in one month—and still get warm responses from each audience. People are people. Their similarities outnumber their differences.

To achieve excellence, though, we must exert a genuine effort to understand the variety of cultures we will inevitably encounter.

The American population has always been a blend of cultures. To continue the success story that has been running for more than two centuries, we must keep looking for the qualities that unite us. We are indeed a nation composed of Anglo-Americans, Italian-Americans, German-Americans, African-Americans, Asian-Americans, Arab-Americans, and many other hyphenated groups. But we have always achieved success as a people by distilling all those hyphenated terms into the two-letter words, *We* and *Us*.

We cannot succeed as a business or a society if we regard people who look and talk like us as "we" and those who look and speak differently as "they." This nation has never been homogeneous. If it had been, America today would be just a bigger, stronger England. But we are not England. We are the United States—a splendid alloy of metals drawn from the whole of the earth, forged on the anvil of hardship and challenge, shaped by the hand of freedom. We can make the alloy even stronger by learning to communicate with our compatriots—in all their varieties—effectively and respectfully.

Fortunately, the 20th century has given us a vast tool kit of technology to facilitate our communication efforts. This technology will enable us to communicate in innovative ways that would astound the people who saw the 19th century give way to the 20th. At that time, the telegraph, the telephone and wireless radio represented the cutting edge of communication technology. In the next chapter, we'll take a quick look at what's ahead in communications technology and how it might affect the businesses of the future.

CHAPTER

12

Power Through Telecommunication

In addition to presenting us with a variety of communication challenges, the 21st century also provides us with a wide range of communication tools. These tools place the entire globe within range of our messages. Our skills at bridging cultural differences are rendered even more useful by the technological advances that make it possible to bridge geographical distances.

We began the 20th century with the telephone and the telegraph, and they were soon followed by radio. We begin the 21st century with a smorgasbord of communication devices.

Hey, Ma Bell! Look what your little black telephone has grown into!

Cellular phones, voice mail and automatic dialing don't even scratch the surface. The 21st century promises to add the dimension of video and computerized data to the traditional voice phone, making it a combination telephone, television and computer—and lots of other things.

The wedding of telephone and computer has a name: Computer Telephone Interface, or CTI.

The new couple will take advantage of digitized data—data transmitted in computer language that can be received by a variety of devices. With the proper equipment, a television set can receive and display computer text and a radio can receive a telephone call.

PREPARING FOR NEW TECHNOLOGIES

These advances are either here now or are just around the corner, and it isn't too early for business leaders to begin preparing for those yet to come. An official of GTE Telephone Operations in Dallas makes these suggestions:

♦ Look at the way your office is wired. The next generation of telecommunications equipment will require the enhanced capacity of fiber optics or other broad-band technologies. Check with your telephone company for suggestions on preparing for these advances.

♦ Inventory your telecommunications equipment. Find out what possibilities exist for present equipment that you may not be aware of. Determine in what ways you might be able to take advantage of services that require greatly enlarged capacity. The videophone could be your next step into the world of telecommunications.

♦ Rethink the way you communicate. You can make a telephone call with your feet on your desk, wearing jogging shorts, or still dripping wet from the shower. The videophone will not be so forgiving. Your dress, your environment, your posture, gestures and facial expressions will all be part of the message. If you use the videophone for sales transactions, you'll need to provide your sales people with additional education to enable them to make maximum use of this new medium.

♦ Look for ways in which you can develop new products and services to take advantage of this technology. Do you have a database that others might pay to use? Could you offer a new service? The opportunities are unlimited.[1]

ALLY OR NUISANCE?

Meanwhile, back in the primitive '90s, the telephone in its present incarnation is one of the strongest allies and greatest nuisances for business people.

Salespeople have learned that the telephone can save on tires and shoe leather. By using a city directory that is cross-indexed for telephone numbers and street addresses, they can locate and reach the people they want to reach. If they spend three minutes on each call, they'll reach 20 prospects an hour, which is hard to do if you're communicating by car, cab or plane.

Executives have learned that conference calls—even without the video dimension—can often eliminate the need for meetings that require people from far-flung places to converge on one spot.

YOU CAN'T FAX A SMILE

The voice phone remains the business person's communications medium of choice while we await the technological refinements that will enable us to debut before the eye of the videophone. And it is a powerful and useful medium.

Fax machines and computer modems have expanded our options for transmitting information, but they still haven't eliminated the need for the immediacy and the intimacy of voice communication. Nor are they likely to eliminate the telephone call—with or without pictures—as a preferred method of getting in touch across distance. Telephone conversations don't have to be typed or punched into word processors. And you can't fax a smile, though you can convey one over the telephone by voice quality.

As a matter of fact, phone calls can often eliminate the need for writing. You'll usually save time for yourself by picking up the telephone instead of the dictaphone. You'll certainly save time for your secretary, which means that you're saving money for your company.

After you've made your call, make notes of what you discussed and keep them organized for ready reference.

With all its advantages, though, the telephone can become a tyrant, monopolizing your time, interrupting your transactions and breaking your concentration. But only if you let it.

Let's look at some ways to make your telephone your ally instead of your nemesis.

THERE'S NO SUBSTITUTE FOR A LIVE VOICE

First, remember that for a good, positive impression by telephone, nothing beats the sound of a live voice that speaks from a knowledgeable mind.

Answering devices can fill in on week-ends and holidays and after hours, but they can't provide the warmth and flexibility of a good telephone receptionist. Nothing is quite so frustrating as to dial a business number and get a synthesized voice that runs down an itemized list of people or departments you can reach if you "touch 1 *now.*" What if the answer is *none of the above?* Your caller has wasted a lot of time listening to the entire list and must still press a button to reach a live person who can route the call to the proper party. Many people resent it when they call long distance and find themselves at the mercy of an answering system.

Even when the videophone marries computer and telephone technology, it's a good bet your callers will welcome a live face and voice to welcome them to your corporate world.

HAVE YOUR CALLS SCREENED

That doesn't mean that you have to be at the beck and call of your telephone at every hour of the day. Your secretary or receptionist can screen your calls, connecting you immediately with the people you need to talk to and holding other calls for you to return at a more convenient time. (It goes without saying that your secretary or receptionist should be articulate, friendly and familiar with your organization.) Designate a certain time of day for returning telephone calls, and at that time answer all the phone calls that have come in. You may have to make adjustments for callers who are several time zones away and exceptions for callers who are in other parts of the world. But a good secretary or receptionist can make those judgments for you.

TAKE CONTROL OF YOUR TIME

When you do place telephone calls, take control of your time. If you have a lot of frequently dialed numbers, an automatic dialer can save you time and money. You can punch a single button to dial the number without having to look it up. If you use a desktop computer, you'll find many software programs that allow quick and easy retrieval of frequently called numbers.

Decide what you want to accomplish with the call and make a list of the important points you want to cover. When you reach your party, get quickly to the heart of the subject, cover the points quickly and end your calls as quickly as you can without being discourteous.

BODY LANGUAGE BY PHONE

When you communicate by sightless telephone, remember that your voice must convey meanings that would be conveyed by a variety of visual clues in a face-to-face conversation. So make full use of the voice qualities covered in Chapter Six: power, pitch, pace, intonation, stress and juncture.

Here's a suggestion: When you speak by telephone, act as if you were speaking face to face. Stand as if you were facing your caller across the room. Smile, just as you would in the presence of the other party. Practice the same body language you would practice in direct conversation. When you do this, your voice will automatically convey the non-verbal nuances.

Your voice conveys more power when you speak from a standing position. It is more natural and less strained when you're not using your neck and shoulder to cradle a telephone. It picks up on smiles and scowls and conveys them through subtle non-verbal clues.

Start your conversation with a rising inflection. This injects a note of warmth and cheerfulness at the outset.

Identify yourself promptly. This applies whether you're the originator or the recipient of the call. If you're calling someone you know, don't assume that your voice will be recognized. Your voice may sound different over the telephone from the way it sounds in person.

IDENTIFY YOURSELF IN FULL

Identify yourself fully, speaking your name slowly and distinctly. Don't say, "Hi George, this is Julie." While you're going into your message, George's mind will be racing through its memory trying to recall all the Julies he has known and trying to decide which one you are.

Assuming that you and George are on first-name terms, say, "Hi George, this is Julie Gladstone at Cosmic Enterprises." If George doesn't recall you immediately, at least he'll know what company you represent.

Speak directly into the mouthpiece, using the natural volume you'd use for a person sitting across the desk from you. This gives you the latitude to vary your volume to suit the message you're trying to convey.

Use the other person's name frequently. This provides a personal touch that compensates for the lack of eye contact.

KNOW WHAT YOU WANT TO ACCOMPLISH

As you talk, keep in mind the reason you're on the telephone:

♦ You want the person on the other end to hear you and understand exactly what you mean.
♦ You want your conversational partner to agree with you, or at least give you a sympathetic ear.
♦ You want to accomplish something. You want the other person to understand what you want done, why it should be done, and when it should be done. And you want your listener to act on what you're saying.
♦ You want to understand the person at the other end of the line.

Think about these objectives each time you speak by telephone. It will help you in planning your calls and in making them both effective and efficient.

CLOSING THE CONVERSATION

If you're the recipient of the call, use questions to determine quickly the purpose of the call and what the caller expects from you. When the call has accomplished its purpose, bring it to a close quickly and courteously. Summarize what you've discussed and the conclusions you've reached. Review the things each party has agreed to do. End with a friendly comment such as "It's been nice talking with you." And let the other person hang up first.

DON'T LET IT BUG YOU

When you're off the phone, be sure you've actually hung up. Laying an open receiver on your desk is like bugging your whole office. And don't assume, while talking on the telephone, that a hand over the mouthpiece will keep your voice from carrying to the other end of the line. Always assume that the other person can hear everything you say.

Technology also means that secrets can pass through electronic cracks. Most executives have little reason to fear electronic eavesdropping, but reasonable precautions should be taken to keep sensitive communications away from prying eyes and ears. Make sure that your incoming and outgoing fax messages are not exposed to unauthorized eyes. Remember that cellular telephones rely on radio transmissions, which can be intercepted by anyone who has a radio tuned to the proper frequency. And hackers consider it a challenge to penetrate corporate computer networks and feast on confidential data. The modern executive need not be paranoid, but it's always wise to have somebody on staff who keeps abreast of the latest technology and can advise you on the best ways to use it effectively while avoiding its pitfalls.

The revolution in telecommunications is so fast and comprehensive that it takes your breath. But remember: The technological advances are simply means of conveying your voice and image across distances. Learn and practice the verbal and non-verbal skills that serve you well in person-to-person interaction. They'll provide the basis for the skills you'll need in tomorrow's high-tech world.

Not all 21st-century communication will require space-age technology to convey messages across oceans and continents.

Much of the work in the business world is still done by people sitting in the same room, often around the same table, sharing information and ideas. The ability to conduct effective meetings is a powerful leadership trait—one we'll explore in the next chapter.

CHAPTER

13

Getting the Most From Meetings

In the 21st century work place, emphasis is on teamwork instead of individual efforts. That means that decisions must be made and problems must be solved by group action. So the effective leader must be skilled at conducting meetings.

Meetings can be caldrons of creativity and fountains of energy, or they can be exercises in wheel-spinning and utter wastes of time. It all depends on how you conduct them.

IS THIS MEETING NECESSARY?

The first step in planning meetings consists of a series of questions. The most important one: "Is this meeting really necessary?"

Often a leader can achieve consensus and teamwork simply by taking a cup of coffee and walking from work station to work station. If you can get the job done that way, why interrupt everyone's routine by calling a formal meeting?

Sometimes meetings are scheduled at regular intervals, and everybody gets together regardless of whether there's anything to talk about. These meetings usually produce little besides yawns.

What's the Purpose?

Assuming that the meeting is necessary, the next question to ask is "What's the basic purpose?" The basic purposes of most meetings fall into one of these categories:

◆ Gathering Information.
◆ Providing information.
◆ Fostering motivation.
◆ Exchanging ideas and solving problems.

Other Questions

Here are some other questions to ask about your meeting:

◆ What is its goal? What do you want to accomplish through this meeting?
◆ Who should attend? Who are the people who would benefit from the meeting or who would contribute the most to it?
◆ Who should conduct it? Who would be most likely to guide the group toward its goal? The highest ranking person in the group isn't necessarily the logical choice for group leader. Often, it's best for executives to take a back seat when serving on cross-functional teams and defer to a team leader who has more knowledge and expertise in the subject being explored.
◆ What procedures and rules will be followed? You may want to stick strictly to parliamentary procedure, with the group voting up or down on each proposal. But it's usually easier to obtain a team's commitment when the decision is reached by consensus.
◆ Where should it be held? The meeting site should be as free of distractions as possible. It should be comfortable, but not too comfortable. And it should have all the resources you need to make your presentation and obtain your decision.
◆ What information should be sent to participants in advance?

Don't wait until you convene the meeting to distribute reading materials. The meeting should be taken up with discussion, not reading. If the participants need certain information to accomplish the purpose of the meeting, distribute that information well in advance of the meeting date. This will make it possible for all participants to be familiar with the material and to give it intelligent discussion.

♦ What audiovisuals do you need for the meeting and who should prepare and present them? Audiovisual presentations should be well planned. Make sure the materials are in the proper order and that the person who presents them is familiar with them.

♦ When should the meeting begin and end? Set definite times for starting and concluding the meeting and stick to them. Late starts are annoying. Meetings that drag on past the allotted time interrupt schedules and result in fidgeting and inattention. Meetings that end abruptly while decisions are still up in the air are frustrating and unsatisfying. Set an agenda. Include only those items that need to be discussed at this meeting. Start on time and end on time.

CHOOSING A LEADER

The choice of a leader is important. A leader must be able to provide strong leadership to keep the meeting on track and to make sure that everyone has an opportunity to participate. When the purpose is to provide information, the leader should take firm control of every facet of the meeting. In such a meeting, the role of the participants is not to provide input but to absorb output. Their function therefore becomes a passive one.

When the purpose is to gather information, solve problems or take advantage of opportunities, you want active participation from the group. In such cases, the leader must be someone who is able to guide a discussion, elicit comments and synthesize the ideas that are advanced. The leader doesn't dominate this type of meeting, but becomes a facilitator.

SEATING ARRANGEMENTS

The purpose of the meeting will determine the best seating arrangement. If you're aiming for an interchange of thought, with everyone encouraged to join in, arrange seats in a circle. If you plan to make use of a panel, arrange the seats in a horseshoe or a T. This focuses attention on those at the head. If the leader is to do all the talking, arrange the seats in rows, as in a theater.

A podium, by elevating you above your audience, will give you greater prominence as a leader, but it will also make you less approachable. A leader who sits around the table with participants or stands at their level is more likely to achieve effective interaction.

If you want to make a formal presentation from a raised platform and later initiate an interchange with participants, there's a way to do it. Step in front of the lectern or—better yet—step down from the platform. Assume an informal pose, and invite discussion.

GROUP BRAINSTORMING

Brainstorming is an effective method for group decision-making. When you embark on brainstorming, these guidelines will help you.

- ♦ *Keep the group small.* The larger the group, the harder it is to obtain consensus. A group of seven to a dozen people usually is the optimum size for decision-making. Such a group is large enough to generate a good supply of ideas and small enough for everyone to provide significant input.
- ♦ *Come prepared.* If you're the leader, you should know what you want to accomplish and should have in mind or at your fingertips the things you need to accomplish it. The partici-

pants will look to you for the basic information and will base their decisions on the facts as you present them.

♦ *Make the purpose clear.* Participants should understand why they're there and what they're expected to accomplish.

♦ *Create a relaxed atmosphere.* People interact better when the mood is informal, the setting is comfortable and they feel that they can relax.

♦ *Don't prescribe; listen.* If you already know the answers, what's the use of calling the meeting? Encourage the group to contribute ideas freely.

♦ *Encourage discussion.* Make it clear that there is no "wrong way" or "right way" and that good decisions result from a thorough examination of all alternatives.

♦ *Discourage ridicule.* Make it clear that criticism is welcome but ridicule is off limits. People should feel free to offer novel ideas without fear of looking foolish. No idea is too exotic for consideration and none is above criticism. In fact, unconventional ideas should be encouraged.

♦ *Prepare for follow-up.* When decisions are reached, make sure that the tasks involved in implementing them are assigned and that the individuals understand and accept their assignments.

STATIC AND DYNAMIC JUDGMENTS

When we hear a new idea advanced, we have a natural tendency to ask, "Will it work? Is it practical?" When we try to answer these questions, we are making *static* judgments.

Static judgments should be suspended during group brainstorming. The proper question is "How might we make this idea work?" Answering that question requires *dynamic* judgments. It stimulates creative thinking. Each dynamic judgment is itself a creative idea, so that one idea triggers several others.

As these ideas are examined, modified and combined, the group progresses toward a consensus. When it reaches that consensus, it will have produced a creative solution, with the feasibility and practicality thoroughly examined.

BRINGING PROBLEMS INTO THE OPEN

Meetings can sometimes be useful in bringing problems into the open. Situations may be simmering just beneath the surface. The leader knows something is wrong but can't quite pinpoint the cause. That's when it's time to sit around the table with staff members and say, "I'd like to hear what's on your minds. What isn't going the way it should be going and what can I do about it?"

If the response is timid, try going to a flip chart. Pick up a pencil and say, "Who'd like to start it off?" The blank page will be like a vacuum demanding to be filled. While you're at the flipchart, keep your back to the staff. They'll feel less intimidated when they don't have to look you in the eye.

Let your staffers talk. Answer any direct questions as well as you can, but remember that your main function is to take notes so that you can review the feedback. At the end of the session, summarize what you've heard, make any necessary corrections and clarifications, and promise to respond to the feedback. Then be sure to keep your promise.

SITUATIONS THAT CALL FOR INTERVENTION

No meeting proceeds smoothly without course corrections. The leader who isn't prepared to intervene may have to stand helplessly while the meeting gets out of hand.

Here are a few situations to watch for and suggestions for dealing with them:

♦ *Group fragmentation.* The group breaks down into a number of private conversations.

This often happens when controversial issues or actions arise and participants begin discussing them among themselves. When this happens, ask the person who has the floor to stop until order has been restored. Call the group to order and ask those who are involved in the individual conversations to share their thoughts in an orderly fashion with the entire group. If the problem persists, call the talkers by name and ask them to join the group. If this doesn't stop the talking, calmly suggest that those involved might want to carry on their discussions in some other place so that the rest of you can get on with the meeting at hand.

- ◆ *Aggressive take-overs.* Sometimes aggressive, extroverted people will try to take over the meeting.

You can exert some control by seating such people next to you and admonishing them through whispers. Another technique is to give the aggressive, outspoken person a formal role in the meeting that will satisfy the need to be heard. If the takeover attempt still seems to be getting out of hand, impose a rigid rule governing the time when each person can speak.

- ◆ *Too many clams.* Some people are timid about speaking up in a group.

You can draw such people into the discussion by asking them specific questions. Then pose follow-up questions to persuade them to elaborate. Assure them that their opinions are valid and welcome.

- ◆ *Uninvited guests.* People may show up who were uninvited and unanticipated.

If it's an open meeting, or if the guests are welcome, acknowledge their presence and invite them to join the discussion. Otherwise, politely (and privately, if possible) ask them to leave.

♦ *Late arrivals.*

Always arrange the room so that the door is to the rear, and leave extra seats near the door. Then let the latecomers straggle in. You don't have to interrupt the meeting to acknowledge their presence.

♦ *Distractions.* Sometimes the setting and room arrangement make it difficult for people to pay attention.

Distractions can be minimized through advance planning. Arrange in advance for a room that has a comfortable temperature. Err on the cool side. The human body is a space heater, and a room full of people will warm up quickly. Try to avoid rooms with outside views—especially if the outside view is a swimming pool, a beach, or some other eye-catching attraction. Make sure the lighting is adequate: Too much is better than too little. Select chairs that are comfortable enough to keep people from squirming but not comfortable enough to lull them to sleep. Make sure that everyone can see and hear you and anyone else in the room.

AFTER THE MEETING

A meeting is productive only if the decisions reached result in concrete and positive actions that lead to the desired goal. The most common failure of meetings is that, when they are over, nothing happens.

You can avoid wasted time and missed opportunities resulting from meetings that get nothing done, if you follow these suggestions:

♦ Make sure all participants understand their assignments.
♦ Distribute the minutes as soon afterward as possible.
♦ Help all participants with their individual assignments.
♦ Check to see that all deadlines are met.
♦ Plan follow-up meetings when they are needed.

I've heard some executives complain that they spend most of their time attending meetings and shuffling papers.

It's true that communication of one type or another tends to monopolize the business day, but then communication is the essence of business. The answer to the challenge is not to stop communicating but to manage communication.

PART THREE

Focusing Your Communications

Focusing On the Right Audience

You can't communicate with everyone in the world, even if you think you have a message everyone ought to hear. Skilled communicators learn to direct their messages toward the audiences they can realistically expect to reach.

Let's make it clear what we mean by an audience. We're not necessarily talking about a group of people sitting in an auditorium listening to you give a speech from a platform. That's just one kind of message and one kind of audience.

For our purposes, your message may take the form of spoken words, written words or graphic representations. It may be delivered in person, on paper, on tape or computer disk, via audiovisual equipment or through electronic transmission.

AIM FOR YOUR AUDIENCE

Your audience is *anyone you want to reach with a message*, whether it be customers, employees, government or the community at large. Identify your audience and aim for it.

For instance:

♦ If you have products and services to sell, you're spinning your wheels if you're directing your sales message to people who have no interest in or need for what you're selling, or who lack the means to buy it.

♦ If your business serves a specific metropolitan area, you're wasting your money and time trying to reach a statewide, regional or national audience.

♦ If your clientele is drawn from a specific professional category, a professional journal or trade publication may be a more effective medium than a general-circulation publication with much wider distribution.

♦ If the communication vehicle you're using doesn't reach the audience you're aiming for, the most compelling of messages will have no effect. The classic example is the billboard that read: "If you can't read, call 1-800-GET HELP." You can't reach illiterate people through written messages. You can't communicate with the blind through videotapes. And you can't communicate with the deaf through audio cassettes.

Aim your communications toward the people who are most likely to be influenced by them.

There are numerous advantages to choosing your audience. Here are some of them:

♦ *You can concentrate all your energies and resources on one focal point.*

When I was a little boy, my brother gave me a small magnifying glass. I knew what its main purpose was. When I held it at a certain distance from an object, it made it look bigger and I could see the object much more clearly. But I soon learned that it had an unsuspected power. It could focus the sun's rays on a tiny spot and, if I held it there long enough, it would burn a hole in the substance on which I focused it.

Communication works on the same principle. Focus your message on the specific audience you want, and you can concentrate and intensify your power. You will be able to gain a clearer, more thorough understanding of the people you want to reach, give them more of yourself, and bring to bear the full power of all you have and all that you are.

♦ *You can provide purpose and direction to your communications efforts.*

In the 21st century, the mass audience is shattering into a myriad of small audiences. There was a time when all America was united during prime time in its attention to three major television networks. We all watched such classics as *Gunsmoke, All in the Family,* and *The Mary Tyler Moore Show.*

Those days are gone. We no longer have a choice of three networks catering to a large, undiversified audience. Instead, we have a smorgasbord of offerings from cable and satellite television, offering network programming, locally produced and syndicated programs, full-length movies, round-the-clock news, round-the-clock weather, round-the-clock current affairs, and a variety of other types of programs. If we can't find what we want among those offerings, we can always go down to the video store and rent a videotape on just about any subject under the sun.

The same is true of the printed media. The nation no longer reads *Time, Life* and *Saturday Evening Post* in unison. Instead, we go to the newsstands in search of the specialty publications targeted toward our particular interests. The armchair traveler can read *National Geographic.* The outdoor person can read *Field & Stream.* Golf enthusiasts can read *Golf Digest.* Epicures can read *Food & Wine.* Dieters can read *Weight Watchers.* There are specialty publications for stamp collectors, coin collectors, boaters, skiers, hang gliders, chess players, bridge players, and Bingo players. There are trade and professional publications for every profession imaginable.

This diversity makes the scattergun approach expensive and ineffective. But it makes it easier for you to pick your target. You can now determine what groups are most likely to respond to your message and choose the media that will reach them.

Direct-mail advertisers have developed this into a science. They know which mailing lists will yield the most prospects for time-share condos, which will yield the most buyers of supplemental health insurance, and which will have the customers lining up for the latest in audio and video equipment.

If you concentrate your efforts on smaller groups with high percentages of prospects, you'll achieve more success at less cost than you'll achieve by appealing to large groups with a low percentage of prospects.

♦ You'll become known by those you would reach.

Successful real-estate agents have developed a sales strategy that can provide a model for other types of communication. They have learned the value of "listing farms." These are neighborhoods or subdivisions that agents adopt as their personal prospecting grounds. The agent tries to become known to the people in that area so that when home owners are ready to sell their property the agent's name will be the first to pop into their minds. Telephone prospecting, canvassing and targeted newsletters all come in the inventory of tools for the listing farmer.

The most successful agents know that a small farm worked intensively will yield better results than a large farm worked less intensively. Why? It's easier to get to know and to be known by the people in the small area.

The underlying strategy applies to all types of communication efforts. Get to know the people you're trying to reach. Become acquainted with their likes and dislikes. And make sure that they are acquainted with you and the ideas you stand for, so that when people make decisions on matters of interest to you, your position will be prominent in their minds and will be clearly associated with your name or the name of your business.

♦ You can save your most valuable asset: time.

Focusing On the Right Audience

When you choose the specific audiences you want to reach and concentrate on just those audiences, you control your time rather than allowing your time to control you.

Again, salespeople provide an example of the futility of trying to reach everyone with your message. Many of them work long hours at a feverish pace and never seem to encounter success. They button-hole everyone they encounter and go into their sales pitches. If you're standing in line with them at the supermarket, they try to sell you. If they run into you at the neighborhood tavern, they try to sell you. If you're sitting beside them on an airplane, they turn on the sales pitch.

Why don't they succeed?

They're not identifying their best prospects and concentrating on them. They're not targeting their audiences. Truly accomplished salespeople identify the prospects who have a logical reason for buying and the resources and authority to make the decision to buy. They spend their time with the people who can give them the response they desire and who are most likely to do so.

The same technique can be followed in non-sales situations. If you're an executive looking about for people to put on your management team, do you spend your time mentoring everyone on your staff? Or do you spot the people with real management potential and work closely with them?

Target your audience, focus your communication, and save yourself time.

♦ *You can practice what you do enough to become really good at it.*

When producers want to work the kinks out of a stage production before exposing it to the scrutiny of Broadway critics, they take it on the road. There, before a variety of crowds in different cities, they can learn what the audiences appreciate. By the time they reach Broadway, they may have dropped certain musical numbers, modified some dialogue and rewritten whole scenes. The performers have learned what facial expressions, body language and voice intonations draw the proper response. They have perfected their timing so that they automatically make the right moves at the right time.

As a professional speaker, I have learned what types of stories draw good response from certain audiences, what kinds of exercises draw them into my presentations, and how to cope with the most common interference I encounter. Thus, I am able to eliminate those stories and exercises that I know won't work and practice those that will work until I can do them automatically. This frees me to concentrate entirely on the people in my audience and the way they are responding to what I'm doing.

This principle holds true with other types of audiences. Just as you become familiar with the house or apartment you live in day after day, so you become acquainted with the people you spend your time with day after day—but only if you concentrate on a limited number of audiences.

♦ *You can multiply your effectiveness by expanding to similar audiences.*

Find a category of customers or clients you click with and stay with it. Look for similar audiences that will respond to similar approaches. This allows you to become better and better at the things that yield success with the people you're trying to reach.

I count on invitations for return engagements, and additional projects for clients, as the backbone of my professional speaking career. If I had to spend a percentage of my time cultivating new clients and developing new approaches for reaching audiences I know nothing about, I would be wasting my most creative energies.

In other types of business, it's more cost-effective to cultivate repeat business with customers whose needs you're familiar with than to be constantly scouting for new business among customers whose needs you don't know as well.

That doesn't mean that you should develop one line of products and stick with it without change. That's a recipe for sure failure in the 21st century. Your customers' needs will be constantly changing. To serve them successfully, you'll have to change with them. But it's much easier to adjust to the needs of customers you know and are already serving than to learn about the changing needs of new customers. It's like trying to follow a moving train. If you're already aboard, a sweeping curve represents only a gentle change of direction, and you feel no great jolt or stress. But if you're running alongside the train at a different pace, trying to grab hold and pull yourself aboard, the curve could jerk you under the wheels and into disaster.

♦ *You can invest your life where you have the highest interest level.*

Most people do best at the things they enjoy doing most. I love speaking to an audience. When I speak to a receptive audience about a subject dear to my heart, I am happiest and at the peak of my effectiveness. To me, public speaking is not work; it's enjoyment. It's play.

Play has often been defined as doing something you enjoy doing. According to this definition, you can play your way through life, and still be very successful, if you choose carefully the audiences you target.

Your audience may be quite different in nature from mine. I'm a speaker and a consultant. Someone else may be a writer, a musician or an actor. We tend to associate audiences with the performing professions, but everyone plays to an audience. If you're a plumber, your audience is the customer who monitors your work and pays your bill. If you're a member of a work-place team, your audience may be your fellow workers. If you're a supervisor, your audience may be the people you supervise. If you're on the management team, your audience may be your colleagues or your staff. If you're a salesperson, your audience is your prospects. If you're in the direct-mail business, your audience may be the people on a mailing list.

CULTIVATE THE RIGHT AUDIENCE

Communication is the life force of every vocation, and your enjoyment of that vocation depends upon the satisfaction you get from the communicating. If you're getting no satisfaction or fulfillment from your efforts, then you may be communicating with the wrong audience. Your interest just isn't there. Find an audience that turns you on, and cultivate it.

How do you do that?

Here are five questions that will help you:

(1) *What do you want to do?*

One of the most common reasons for the failure of communication efforts is that the people who initiate them don't know what they want to accomplish. They may have a general idea of what they want, but their goals are so vague that no one can understand them. Therefore, they have no logical audience.

Be specific. What do you want to accomplish? One way to focus your thoughts on that question is to write one concise sentence describing precisely what you want to do. This will lead you to the next question:

(2) *Who can help you get it done?*

The best audience for your communication is the one that can give you the most help in doing what you want to do. If you've just bought a stereo that delivers sound from only one speaker, you won't get it fixed by telling your tale of woe to the entire neighborhood. You'll achieve it by describing your problem to the person who sold you the stereo.

If you want to start a new Department of Innovation in your company, you don't take your idea to the people in the company cafeteria. You take it to the executive who has the authority to make the decision, or to someone who is in position to influence the people in authority.

186

If you want to get maximum performance from your sales team, teach the members to target their audiences. Some of the hardest-working salespeople I've met in my seminars were dismal failures because they hadn't learned to target their audiences. They were articulate, personable and knowledgeable about the products they sold. But they didn't pick their prospects well. They wasted most of their time talking to people who could not buy what they had to sell. When they learned how to determine who could best make the decisions they wanted them to make, they were able to sell more in less time, and with less effort, and often at a higher profit.

Don't look for the person who will listen sympathetically. Look for the person who can give you the results you want.

(3) *Who would want to help you do it?*

People do things for *their* reasons, not yours. If you want people to help you accomplish what you want to accomplish, look for the people who have the strongest reasons for helping you.

The salesperson who sold you the defective stereo has a stronger reason for helping you than does the manager of the store's garden department. Why? Because the stereo salesperson stands to lose if you return the item for a refund, and if you take your repeat business elsewhere.

A direct-mail corporate client of mine put zip into its sales performance by following my advice and targeting the audience that had reason for wanting its product.

I looked over the company's very specialized product line and suggested that it rent a mailing list of people who had bought similar products from other companies.

At first management demurred. The specialized lists cost more than the lists they were renting.

Yes, I pointed out, but the specialized lists contained the names of the people who would help them: the people who would like to buy their products.

Management took my advice and was delighted at the results.

The more expensive lists produced a higher percentage of people who wanted to buy the products. Sales improved dramatically.

The advice delivered two millenniums ago from the hillside in Galilee remains valid: Don't "cast your pearls before swine." In other words, don't waste your breath telling your story to people who feel no need to hear it. Go to the people who are likely to give you the response you desire.

(4) *Why would an audience listen to you?*

Remember that this is the age of communication. We are bombarded with messages everywhere we go. So why should anyone listen to your message in particular?

Answer that question as candidly and objectively as you can. Don't be overly modest and don't be egotistical about it. What qualifications do you have to ask people to do what you want them to do?

The answer may lie in your position of authority, the influence you exert over your audience, or the specialized knowledge that you have and they need. It may lie in your superb eloquence—your strong persuasive powers. Or it may lie in fortuitous circumstances.

(5) *How accessible is this audience?*

If you want to run a full-page ad in *The Wall Street Journal,* it's going to cost you plenty. The *Journal's* huge, widely dispersed readership is accessible only to those who have the resources to market nationally. You can reach *Journal* readers with your message, if you're willing to fork over the cash or if you can persuade the editors that your message is worth printing in the news or opinion columns. But if you run a neighborhood grocery, they're inaccessible to you, for all practical purposes, because even though you can reach them with your message, they can't respond by buying your products.

Even the readership of the daily newspaper serving your city may be inaccessible to you if you draw your clientele from only a small corner of the metropolitan area. But many metropolitan papers carve their circulation areas into smaller segments and publish zoned editions to serve them. These zoned editions offer attractive advertising rates to merchants who need only to reach readers within their areas of coverage.

There are other ways of reaching targeted audiences. Do you know of other people who have contact with the audience you want to reach? If so, do they have reason to help you contact that audience? Book or magazine publishers may be selling printed materials regularly to an audience you want to reach. They may find it worthwhile to publish something you've written to appeal to their audience. Talk show hosts on radio and television are always looking for guests who have something interesting to say to their audiences.

People with common interests often form associations, and these organizations can serve as vehicles for reaching their members. Such organizations frequently publish newsletters, newspapers and magazines that accept articles from outsiders. Don't overlook the possibility of speaking to these groups at chapter meetings or at conventions.

Analyze a potential audience and determine how accessible it is. If it can be reached without overtaxing your resources and if it appears likely to respond to your message, go for it.

EVALUATE YOUR AUDIENCES

Once you have narrowed your choice of audiences through these five questions, your next step is to evaluate them to see which you want to reach.

Here are some criteria for evaluating them:

♦ *The targeted audience should have the power to do what you want it to do.*

The executive vice president for operations may have the *authority* to authorize the purchase of a fleet of trucks, but she may lack the *power* because the board of directors failed to budget enough money for the purchase.

Your boss may have the *authority* to grant you a raise, but someone higher in the organization may have the *power* to overrule the decision. If you're unhappy with your 5% raise, to whom do you appeal? Your boss, who may have recommended 10%, or your boss's superior, who might have cut the recommendation in half?

♦ *The audience should know that it needs to hear what you have to say.*

If the audience is not aware of its need to listen, it probably won't listen. You can take the time and make the effort to educate it about its need to listen, but that will take an extra investment of time and energy. Could that investment be made more productively elsewhere?

♦ *The audience should* want *to hear what you have to say.*

An audience must be able to see the benefit in the message you're sending, and must be ready to hear it. Had I gone to Erfurt, Germany, in 1983 to speak on the subject of entrepreneurship, I probably would have spoken to an empty house, and very likely would have received an official government invitation to leave the country.

But when I went there in 1993, on the third anniversary of German reunification, some 500 business owners drove through bad weather for up to six hours, and paid hard-earned Deutchsmarks to hear me speak. Why?

Because Erfurt was a part of communist East Germany in 1983, and communism suppressed private enterprise. Learning how to succeed in a market economy was useless information to people who did not live in a market economy. By 1993, though, Erfurt was part of a unified Germany, and business people who had grown up grappling with the communist system now needed to learn the ropes of capitalism. They were hungry for what I had to say.

I found similar enthusiasm in Luxembourg, the small principality that serves as the capital of the European Community. With opportunities beckoning in this populous common market, more than 800 European business leaders showed up at the EC's Parliament House, where my speech was translated into six languages.

Impressive things happen when the right message reaches an audience that wants to hear it. When the audience isn't ready to listen, you can save your breath.

When John Kennedy took office as president, he challenged his fellow citizens with these words:

Ask not what your country can do for you; ask what you can do for your country.

The people were ready to listen; it was something they wanted to hear.

When Jimmy Carter spoke of a national "malaise," and called for individual sacrifices, the people were not ready to listen; it wasn't something they wanted to hear.

It takes extraordinary eloquence to overcome an audience's unwillingness to listen. Even the great Winston Churchill had to sit out of power for six years following World War II, because the people he had led to victory didn't want to hear his message that the Tory party was best fitted to lead the postwar reconstruction.

♦ *The audience should fit into your life's goals.*

If you know who you are and where you're going, an occasional detour to reach out to an audience might help to fulfill some of your goals. However, one detour can lead to another until you find that you're investing your best resources in audiences that are not leading you toward your goals.

Using these criteria, you should be able to determine which audience has the best potential for giving the response you desire for the least amount of time and resources invested.

ONE MORE QUESTION

Now there's one other question to ask: ***Are you the best person to present this message to this audience?***

In some cases, it might be more productive for you to get someone else to say what you want said. I have turned down many speaking engagements because I knew there were others who could deliver a particular message to a given audience much more productively than I could. Remember, as a communicator, your goal is not to stroke your own ego, but to get the response you desire. If others can do that better for you, look for a way to get them to do it.

Focusing on the right audience is just the first step. To achieve the desired results, the right message has to reach the right audience. So it's necessary to focus your message for the audience you have in mind. The next chapter will show how it's done.

Focusing Your Message

You know what audience you want to reach and what response you want. Now your task is to focus your message.

Focusing your message means finding the precise message to persuade your audience to do what you want it to do, then presenting the message in the most appealing way.

WATCH THE MAIN TITLES

The best examples of such targeting at work are the "main titles" television shows use to lock in their audiences. These are the 15- to 20-second grabbers at the beginning of each show. They're designed to make you pause in the midst of your channel hopping to watch the opening scenes from the program, or to prevent you from flipping to another channel to sample its wares. The networks reason that if they can get you to watch for just a few seconds, they stand a better chance of hooking you for the duration of the show.

Networks will pay well into six figures for a good "main title," because they know that the millions spent on producing the show will go down the tube if the viewers don't stick around to watch. The bigger the audience, the more commercials they can sell and the more they can charge for them.

What the networks look for in main titles, you should be looking for in the way you launch your messages. Here's what a main title is supposed to do:

♦ Gain attention immediately and hold it.
♦ Introduce the subject to be covered.
♦ Set the tone, pace and mood for the show.
♦ Introduce the characters and convince the audience that they are good people to spend time with—people you can identify with.
♦ Dispel any fears the audience has about watching the show.

Take a couple of evenings to relax with your remote control and watch the main titles carefully. Note the techniques and think about ways you can adapt them to your communications, whether you're giving a speech, trying a case in court, writing a memo to your staff or proposing marriage to your true love.

FIVE BASIC STEPS IN FOCUSING

You can follow five basic steps in focusing your message for maximum effect: 1) Target your subject; 2) Collect all the materials you need; 3) Select the materials you will use; 4) Let it ripen in your mind; 5) Organize your message.

Target Your Subject

Decide what you want your audience to do in response to your communication. If you're making a speech, do you want to have your audience laughing, crying, patting each other on the back or charging into the field bent on setting new sales records? You might want them to do several of those things, but one objective should predominate. Otherwise, your audience will be confused.

Remember that the subjects of communications are related to needs and wants and the satisfaction of needs and wants. If you don't need or want anything, there's no reason to communicate. Sometimes, communication itself is the principal need. If you've been isolated from human companionship for a long time, you have a strong and urgent need to communicate. In the work place, communication usually centers on the things needed to accomplish the job and produce a product or service at a profit.

If you build your message on the needs of your audience, you are choosing the strongest possible subject. If you can address people's needs in a way that gives hope that you'll satisfy them, you immediately get their attention. Identify people's needs and wants, then convince them that the actions you propose will satisfy them, and you'll get the response you desire.

STICK TO SUBJECTS YOU KNOW

You may have heard the story about the deacon who attended a meeting called to decide whether the church should spend the money to buy a new chandelier. The deacon listened to the arguments, then rose to have his say.

"Brethren," he began, "I'm firmly opposed to this church spending its money on a chandelier, for three solid reasons: First, nobody in the church knows how to spell it; second nobody here can play it, and third, what this church needs is more light."

On another occasion, a man who professed to be an authority on every subject walked into a barber shop and saw a scruffy owl perched on top of a cabinet. The man proceeded to belittle the taxidermist for doing such a poor job of stuffing the bird. He held forth on the finer points of ornithology, noting how the owl's wings hung at the wrong angle, its head was askew and the color of the feathers indicated that the taxidermist had touched up his work with some cheap hair coloring.

When the man had finished talking, all eyes were on the owl. The bird blinked a couple of times, stretched its wings, then flew to the opposite side of the room.

Both stories illustrate the truth of the adage: It's better to keep your mouth shut and let people think you're ignorant than to open it and remove all doubt.

If you're a speaker or facilitator, your audience rating goes up in direct proportion to your knowledge of the subject. I'm often invited to speak to audiences on subjects about which I know little or nothing. Unless I can easily learn enough about the subject to speak intelligently on it, I suggest another topic, recommend a fellow speaker, or decline the invitation. I respect both my audience and my career too much to run all over the world showing my ignorance.

Usually, the subjects you know the most about are the ones that reflect your deepest interests. You'll always be more impressive and more effective when you're communicating about subjects in which you have a vital interest.

In the work place, too, it's important that you know what you're talking about. Good leaders know where their expertise begins and ends. They don't mind sharing their expertise with the people they lead, but they're not too proud to admit it when they don't know the answers. Leadership in the 21st century doesn't consist of knowing all the answers. It consists, rather, of knowing where to go or whom to go to for the answers.

SPEAK TO SUBJECTS THAT ARE MANAGEABLE

Don't take on a subject that you can't deal with adequately in a reasonable amount of time. This often requires nothing more than determining what people want to know or what they need to know, and confining your message to those points. Or it may require that you break your subject into manageable sub-topics and deal with them one at a time.

Don't be like the mother of 6-year-old Robyn, when asked, "Mom, where did I come from?"

Mom proceeded to explain to Robyn all the details of human bi ology: how the mother's body produces the egg, which descends from the ovary down the Fallopian tube to the uterus, where it meets the sperm cells from the father, which have swum up through the vagina until they reach the egg, penetrate it and fertilize it; how the genetic code works to construct an entirely new human out of the seeds of the two parents; how the cells divide to form an embryo, which develops within the placenta, and how at full term a fully developed baby appears.

By the time Mom was finished, Robyn's eyes were glazed.

"Does that explain it to you?" asked Mom.

"I guess so," yawned Robyn. "But my friend Todd says he came from Florida."

Mom could have skipped the details and answered Robyn's question in one word. Instead, she tried to compress a biology textbook into one lesson and she overextended herself.

We often do that in our communications. We try to tell everything in one session. In the process we confuse our listeners and lose their attention.

Don't try to tell it all in one sitting. If your subject is a broad one, break it down into manageable segments and focus on one segment at a time.

For Robyn, it was enough for the time being to know that she came from Virginia. She could be told later how her mother carried her for approximately nine months within her body. A later conversation could deal with conception. We learn in small increments. So it's best to communicate in small, focused increments.

Collect All the Materials You Need

The more you know about a subject, the more forcefully you can present your message. So your first step is research.

On some subjects you may already be up to speed. Your research will need only to fill in the nooks and crannies and to refresh your memory.

On other subjects, you'll need to do extensive research. Cast a broad net. You'll want to focus your information later, but initially your task is to gather all the facts that you can. Assume nothing. Be sure of your facts. This is especially true if you're criticizing someone.

As you gather information, keep in mind the main thrust of your communication. Assemble everything you need to make a strong case. Collect quotes, specific examples, research data, and anything else that will support your position or help you clarify it. Gather more information than you plan to use, so you can select the strongest pieces of information.

Then study the material. You won't be able to deliver your message effectively until you get it off the page or out of your word processor and into your mind.

Select the Materials You Will Use

The most effective materials are those most likely to get the response you want. If your object is to persuade a prospect to become your customer, look for the thing you offer that will provide the most powerful motive to do business with you instead of someone else. This is what advertising copywriters call the "unique selling proposition."

Whether you're trying to make a sale, inspire greater productivity, or persuade your true love to meet you at the altar, look for your unique selling proposition and concentrate on that.

In most forms of communication, you can count on making only one good point. I have found it helpful to boil down the most important point I want to make in a concise sentence that expresses it concisely. That's true whether I'm dictating a letter or memo, preparing a speech, writing a book or structuring an action plan for a prospective client. Once I have a clear focus on what I want to say, I'm better able to convey the message to the audience.

Having selected your most compelling point, look for the materials and arguments that present it in the clearest light and support it most emphatically. If there's something that needs clarifying and explaining to your audience, find the simplest, most comprehensible way to explain it. Select the information, materials and arguments that add the most credibility to your main point. If you know your audience, you can select the supportive materials you feel it will find most convincing. Keep cutting away the fluff until only the essential points, ideas, arguments and supporting data remain.

Let It Ripen in Your Mind

Horace, the ancient Roman poet and satirist, uttered a truth that people of all ages have learned to their chagrin: "Once a word has been allowed to escape, it cannot be recalled."

That's why it's wise to sleep on important communications. Give them time to ripen in your mind. Give your intuitive mind a chance to examine them and respond to them. How will it sound to the audience you're trying to reach? Are you sure that's the best way you can say it? Are you sure the results it will bring are the results you want?

We've all had the experience of dropping a letter in the mail and almost immediately regretting that we mailed it. We've all said things in anger that we immediately wish had remained unsaid. We've all gotten into arguments and, hours and days later, thought of just the right words that might have made the point we were trying to make.

There are times when you have to respond on the spur of the moment. But why respond in haste when it isn't necessary? Sometimes, when I have a very important letter to write, I will dictate a draft. Then I will let it incubate for several days, using that time to question everything I have said. If it's really important, I will test my statements on some people whose judgments I value. Once I feel that I have really digested what I want to say, I dictate a final draft. This process has helped me to avoid the consequences of poor communication in many situations.

Organize Your Message

Every communication springs from a process of organizing. You have to organize your ideas, then express them in sentences, which consist of words assembled in an organized fashion.

Casual conversation is only loosely organized. We speak spontaneously as ideas form in our minds, giving very little thought to how we will express ourselves.

This loose-jointed method of assembling and expressing ideas works very well when we're making small talk. But when it comes to expressing important ideas, much more preparation is necessary. That's why the U.S. president's staff will spend weeks researching, writing and rewriting a State of the Union message. No president would go before Congress and deliver a State of the Union message spontaneously, off the cuff.

So when you have something important to say, whether it's giving directions to your staff, giving a performance appraisal to an employee or giving a report to the Board of Directors, it pays to organize.

Here are some tips for organizing your communications:

♦ *Organize around your most compelling points.*

Recall the two stories I told earlier in this chapter, about the deacon at the church meeting and the owl in the barber shop.

Did you chuckle when you read the deacon's words, ". . . what this church needs is more light"?

By itself, there's nothing funny about the line. If I had begun my story with that statement, you wouldn't have chuckled. The organization made the difference. Every sentence in the story led up to the punchline.

And in the story about the owl, what if I had revealed in the first sentence or two that the owl was alive and not stuffed? The effect would have been lost.

The principle applies whether you're telling a joke or negotiating a merger. Your most compelling point has more impact when you set it up. That doesn't mean that it has to come at the end of your message, like the punchline of a joke. But your whole communication should be organized with a view toward presenting your compelling point in the most powerful way.

Sometimes the most powerful way is to state boldly and clearly what you want at the outset of your message, then follow with statements that explain and support it. This grabs the audience's attention and makes it receptive to the supporting points that follow. This approach works best when you know the audience will be friendly toward your ideas and will perhaps be enthusiastic about them.

If you expect audience resistance, the best approach might be to start on common ground. Begin by stating the ideas that you know your audience will agree with. Then gradually, logically, build toward your compelling point.

This technique can work, too, when you want to build suspense toward a dramatic climax—as when you're unveiling a revolutionary new product.

At times you might state your most compelling point repeatedly throughout the message, each time using supportive material to set it up.

The number of ways to organize your message is limited only by your imagination. But for maximum impact, you have to organize.

◆ *Use three major components.*

Regardless of which type of organization you use, your message will consist of three fundamental parts: an introduction, a body and a conclusion.

The Introduction

The introduction should be an attention-getter. Newspaper and magazine writers are taught that the most important paragraph in any story is the first paragraph: the lead. The headline writer usually derives the headline from the lead. Readers may be drawn to the story by the headline and accompanying illustrations, but it's the lead that determines whether they'll read on or go to the next headline.

An introduction has to be more than an attention-rouser. It must lead the audience directly into the body of the message. If it doesn't do that, you're likely to find yourself in the position of the absent-minded pastor who visited another church and was impressed by the opening words of the pastor's sermon: "I spent the best years of my life in the arms of another man's wife." The congregation was immediately awake, and ready for the next line: "She was my mother."

The absent-minded pastor decided to use it on his own congregation.

"You know, I spent the best years of my life in the arms of another man's wife," he began. The audience came to shocked attention. And the pastor forgot the next line. After several seconds that seemed like an eternity, he finally stammered, "I can't remember who she was."

I sometimes hear speakers open by saying "Sex! Now that I have your attention, I want to talk about. . . ."

That introduction may be effective if your subject is, indeed, sex. But if it's a report to stockholders on your third-quarter performance, you're still stuck with the task of introducing your *real* subject.

Somebody somewhere in the dim reaches of time began telling students in Public Speaking 101 that a speech should begin with a good joke. The first cave man to rally the clan to an elephant hunt probably started his speech with an elephant joke, and thus was born the cliche.

The 21st century is a good time to scrap that advice. A good joke at the start of a speech may get the attention of the audience and put it in a good mood, but it gives you a tough act to follow. Unless the joke has direct relevance to your most compelling point, its effect is lost as soon as the laughter dies. You now have to figure out how to direct the attention away from the jollity and toward your central message.

A good introduction must always alert an audience to the fact that what is about to be said is something it should hear. If it contains a humorous note, fine. But the humor should oil the skids that lead into the main body of the communication. If it doesn't, you'll skid smack into a wall of inattention.

The Main Body

The main body of communication presents the most compelling point in the clearest and most stimulating light. It must make your message *SING*. That means it must do four things:

(1) *Scintillate.* That's a five-dollar word for sparkle, excite and entertain.

(2) *Inform or instruct.* The audience should go away with the feeling that it has gained new knowledge, new understanding or new insight.

(3) *Nudge toward action or agreement.* In other words, persuade or influence.

(4) *Give inspiration.*

A strong communication doesn't perform these four functions one at a time. Each function is interwoven throughout the body of the talk. If you try to progress from scintillating to informing to persuading to inspiring, you'll leave your audiences behind. They'll listen so long as you're being entertaining, but when you switch from a humorous to a serious vein, they'll tune you out.

If you're going to use humor (and it's an effective form of entertainment), sprinkle it throughout your communication. An effective technique is to make a point, then wrap it up with a humorous illustration. The illustration adds to the impact of the point and makes it memorable.

The three-point body is the simplest form of organization. Decide how you want to present your most compelling point and use the other two points to set it up or explain it. In one type of organization, Point One might be your most compelling point. Point Two could explain it and Point Three would persuade the audience to take action on it.

Suppose you've had a good quarter and you're announcing the results to your employees. You might organize your communication this way:

(1) *Performance-related bonuses are 20% higher this month.* **(Your most compelling point).**

(2) *This is because of the success of our continuous quality-improvement process, which resulted in a reduction in defects from 25 per thousand units to 9 per thousand. This meant lower production costs and a healthy rise in net earnings.* **(Supporting point).**

(3) *If the employees can bring defects down to the level of 4 per 1,000, they can look forward to even larger bonuses next quarter.* **(Persuading to act).**

Suppose you're introducing your newest product line to a group of retail dealers. Your organization might be something like this:

(1) *Most young people who are just starting households are well-educated with sophisticated tastes in home furnishings.* **(Setting up.)**

(2) *However, few of them have the income to buy costly originals, and many of them are looking for furnishings that will be able to survive their child-rearing years.* **(Explaining.)**

(3) *Our new line of furniture has the look of authentic originals; yet it is made of inexpensive materials designed to resist stains, scratches and tears.* **(Unique Selling Proposition.)**

Experiment with different arrangements. But always aim to present your most compelling point in its most convincing setting.

The Conclusion

A conclusion does more than ring down the curtain on your message. It is your last opportunity to make your message accomplish what you set out for it to accomplish.

A good conclusion can accomplish these things:

♦ *Reinforce what you have said.*

One good way to do this is to summarize the main points briefly. Distill the essence of your message into three or four short, memorable sentences so that the audience leaves with your ideas ringing in its ears.

♦ *Invite people to act.*

Salespeople know that their presentation isn't complete until they've asked for the order. Your message isn't complete until you've told your the people in your audience clearly, precisely and persuasively what you want them to do.

♦ *Inspire your audience.*

You might do this with a challenging question, a glowing promise, or a strong statement of your most compelling point.

One caveat: Be sure that you're inspiring them to do what you want them to do.

A group of hunters who wanted to hunt doves on a farmer's property sent Charlie to the door to ask the owner's permission. The farmer agreed, but asked a favor in return: "I have a sick mule down in the pasture, and I need to put him out of his misery. But I just don't have the heart to do it. Would you mind taking care of that sad chore for me?"

Charlie agreed, but when he saw the sad old mule standing by the farmer's faithful milk cow, he too lacked the heart to dispatch the animal. So he told his fellow hunters: "That farmer was so rude, I can't believe it. He called us every name in the book and told us to get off his property pronto or he'd shoot the tires off the van. I think we need to teach this guy a lesson. Judy, you've got your gun loaded; why don't you shoot his mule."

Judy took careful aim, and quickly and mercifully dispatched the ailing animal.

By this time, Hank had taken his gun out of the van and loaded it.

"I'm fighting mad too," he fumed as he took careful aim and squeezed the trigger. "I think I'll kill his cow!"

Charlie's message had inspired his listeners to act—but in a way that he hadn't bargained for.

♦ *Set the stage for future communications.*

Sometimes your entire purpose can't be accomplished with one communication. So your conclusion can prepare your audience for what's to come:

". . . So as you can see, our proposed new facility will have minimal impact on the air quality for the region. We are confident that the same will be true of water quality, and we will submit the appropriate data as soon as our environmental analysis is complete."

YOUR HOUSE OF COMMUNICATION

Like a house under construction, a communication does not emerge suddenly fully formed. A house starts with a foundation. The framework is erected on this foundation. Then follow the walls, roof and floor. Partitions are erected. Finally come the finishing touches: paint, plaster, wallpaper, carpeting and fixtures.

A communication in any form must start with a foundation. It is built upon a central purpose.

The framework consists of an outline—the main points listed in the order that they will be presented.

The outline is partitioned into an introduction, body and conclusion. Into this shell, you move your information, ideas, arguments and explanations.

The introduction is the entrance to your house. It should be inviting and functional. It should lead smoothly and conveniently to the other areas of the building, with a theme that is echoed throughout.

The main body is your living space. You'll take your audience through your living room and den for entertainment. You'll present food for thought in your dining room and kitchen. You'll go into the library for information. The information, ideas, arguments and explanations form the furnishings. Your anecdotes, images and illustrations form the decor.

The conclusion takes your guests out of the building and into the garden of inspiration and contemplation, where they can reflect upon the things they encountered within and apply them in their own lives.

Let's suppose that you're in charge of drumming up attendance for the annual convention of your trade association. You want to send a letter that will motivate people to attend. Here's how you might outline it:

I. Introduction
  A. Give the date and site of the convention.
  B. Cite the advantages of the timing.
  C. Paint an attractive picture of the setting.
II. Main Body
  A. Give details of the program.
  B. Show the advantages to the attendee.
  C. Give details of hotel rates and registration fees.
III. Conclusion
  A. Suggest that the convention be combined with vacation plans.
  B. End with a hearty invitation to attend.

Following the outline, you might compose the following letter:

Dear [Name of Member]:

Come join us in New Orleans April 15–18 for the annual convention of the National Plant Nursery Association. At this time of year, the historic old city puts on its spring finery and reveals what a delightful place it can be. The charming Bourbon Orleans Hotel is an ideal base from which to explore the exciting French Quarter and to sample the food and entertainment in this city that blends the cultures of America, Europe and Africa.

Our featured speaker will be Dr. Rose la Fleur, professor of botany at Tulane University, who will show us blooms from the three new varieties of roses she has developed and will tell how you can make them a money-making part of your inventory for next spring.

Dr. I. B. MacIntosh, professor of computer science at Louisiana Tech, will demonstrate how computers can help you build more profitability into your business at minimum capital expense. A panel of your fellow members will share with you some of the ways they have used computers to enhance profits.

J. P. Hedgerow, president of Hedgerow and Boxwood Nurseries of Richmond, Virginia, will describe ways of expanding your business by developing and nurturing new market areas. A complete program is enclosed.

There'll be opportunities for golf and tennis, of course, at the city's splendid recreational facilities, and a chance to partake of the food, entertainment and excitement of the famed French Quarter.

We still have rooms available for $90 a night per couple, and registration is only $250 per member and $125 for spouse or companion.

What an excellent opportunity to combine a business trip with a pleasure excursion! I know you'll want to attend. If you'll return the enclosed registration form by May 15, we'll hold a place for you. See you there!

Daisy Larkspur
Convention chairman

The introduction opens with the most compelling point: the time and place of the national convention. It paints an inviting scene and beckons the reader into the body of the letter for more information.

The body provides the pertinent information: a list of the topics and speakers with suggestions on how they can help the business owner, and a summary of hotel rates and registration fees.

The conclusion suggests that the member combine the business trip with vacation plans and asks that the registration form be returned. The writer tells the recipient what she wants done and when she wants it done.

A message, of course, can't accomplish its purpose until it has been presented to the receiver. The next chapter will help you focus your presentation.

CHAPTER

16

Focusing Your Presentation

Once you've focused on your *audience* and have focused your *message*, it's necessary to turn your attention toward your *presentation.* Your presentation is the means by which you deliver your message to your audience. Focusing it requires that you *choose the right medium, use it to best advantage* and *aim for the right response.*

Let's say that you're a musician and you were called upon to provide some diversion for a group of business executives after a heavy round of conferences.

You chose to play Debussey's *Afternoon of a Faun,* and it bombed.

There was nothing wrong with the message. It was the same great composition that has thrilled audiences for a century or more. There was nothing wrong with the audience—a group of cultured business executives gathered in the lounge of a top-flight hotel. But the presentation wasn't focused. It used the wrong medium and you used it to poor advantage. It also aimed for the wrong response.

The medium was a tenor banjo—the wrong strings for Debussey. If you had been presenting a medley of tunes from *Showboat,* you would have been using the medium to good advantage. But for Debussey, a concert piano would have been more appropriate.

Even had you given an accomplished piano performance, your communication would still have fallen short. After a grueling round of conferences, these executives were interested in some lively stimulation, and this was the night for game six of the World Series. The executives were gathered around a large-screen set watching the baseball action. They might have enjoyed a round or two of "Take Me Out to the Ball Game," and some appropriate fanfare during exciting moments of play. But nobody wants to listen to Debussey when there are two outs, the tying run is on second and the count is three and two. Debussey induces reverie. The response you were after was excitement.

Whatever message you're trying to deliver, no matter how skillfully you deliver it and no matter how appropriate the audience, if the presentation isn't properly focused, it will flop.

A WIDE SELECTION OF MEDIA

The plethora of media available in the 21st century makes it technically easy to reach an audience two feet or two continents away. You can send a note via computer network to your secretary in the reception area or you can send a fax to your company's geologist in the rain forests of Indonesia.

But that doesn't mean that your message will be heard or heeded. The globe is saturated with messages, and each of us has to decide which one we'll pay attention to for the moment. A television ad aimed at business executives is likely to receive little attention if it's aired during the mid-morning hours. An advertisement for a Rolls Royce, no matter how skillfully crafted, is not likely to generate showroom traffic if it's published in Boy's Life.

WHICH MEDIUM IS BEST?

Message senders must decide which media are the most effective avenues to their audiences under the given circumstances. A good presentation by itself doesn't assure success. It succeeds only when it gets the desired response from the targeted audience.

Focusing Your Presentation

How do you determine which medium to use?
Here are some suggestions:

♦ **Choose a medium that fits the image you want to project.**

The medium should reflect your personality or the corporate image. You don't present your annual report in a comic-book format. You don't advertise your designer originals in *Mad* magazine. Take the time to browse through some magazines. Note which companies advertise in which magazines, and how the messages vary from publication to publication.

♦ **Choose a medium that fits the audience you want to reach.**

To make that choice, you need to know what kind of people are in your audience. You need to know what they read, what television programs they watch, what radio stations they listen to, their tastes in music and clothes, their reaction to visual messages, their accessibility to the telephone and the types of mail they get.

Telemarketing, for instance, might work fine if your audience is working couples who can be reached and sold at home. But if your audience consists of business executives who must be reached and sold at their offices, telemarketing might be disastrous.

♦ **Choose a medium that fits your purpose in sending the message.**

If you're soliciting small donations from a mass audience, a form letter may be effective. But if you're looking for big-ticket contributors, willing to contribute on the order of $10,000 or more, steer clear of the form letter. Personal visits are a must.

A number of factors should govern your choice of a medium. Cost is important. The results must be worth the expenditure. Simplicity is another. If the medium depends upon extensive use of graphics and you lack the expertise or the resources to prepare the graphics, it's not the medium for you. Your plans for follow-up will also affect your choice. But the most important consideration is whether the medium fits your purpose.

♦ *Choose a medium that fits your message.*

If you're trying to explain to your employees why wage increases are going to be cut back or to your stockholders why you're skipping the quarterly dividend, don't send your message in a slick, four-color brochure. You can't plead austerity while you're traveling first class. Ask yourself: How complex is the message? What is its tone and nature? What will the medium say about the message?

♦ *Choose a medium that fits the occasion.*

Once a newspaper editor carefully planned his editorial page for Christmas day so that it would be inspirational to those of the Christian and Jewish faiths. He wrote an editorial that called attention to the traditions of Hannukah as well as those of Christmas, and pointed out the significance of the events celebrated by each festival. He chose Biblical passages that are respected by both faiths. What he didn't do was choose the editorial cartoon for the facing page. The cartoon was chosen by another editor. It featured a caricature of Menachem Begin, then prime minister of Israel, flying over conquered Arab territories with a scroll in his hands and shouting "Torah, Torah, Torah." The presentation was a clever criticism of Israel's actions in annexing the Golan Heights from Syria. It alluded to the famous war cry of the Japanese pilots attacking Pearl Harbor: "Tora, Tora, Tora."

But the cartoon was preeminently the wrong medium for the wrong occasion. Jewish readers interpreted it as an affront to their sacred writings, delivered at a particularly inappropriate time of the year.

Presentations can be poorly targeted in less emotional ways. Many meeting planners lose sight of circumstances and attitudes

214

when they arrange their programs. In the early morning, after a night of heavy partying, it's no time to hit an audience with a complex audio-visual presentation. In the late evening, after a heavy meal complete with dessert, it's no time to schedule a heavy lecture on economics.

The right medium for any presentation is the medium that will convey most effectively the message at the time it is to be sent to the audience. The mood of the audience, the tempo of the presentation, the nature of the occasion and the nature of the audience's activity at the time of the presentation are all major considerations in choosing the right medium.

♦ *Choose a medium that has the capacity to convey the message you wish to present.*

This is a factor too often overlooked in the business world. An executive applies for a $125,000 a year position and sends off a one-page photocopied resume. The medium is inadequate. The resume for such a position must showcase the applicant's capabilities, and it must reflect quality and class.

We often overestimate the power of written communication, however. A client once noted that his semi-skilled workers were leaving his company for other companies that paid only marginally better wages and offered far less in employee benefits. When benefits were factored in, they were earning less in their new jobs than they earned in the old ones.

"Do they know that?" asked one of my associates, who was consulting with the company.

"Sure," replied the executive. "We give them a booklet that explains it all as soon as they're hired."

The consultant checked into it and found that few employees actually read the booklet, and few who read it could understand it. The booklet was inadequate for the task.

Each medium has its strengths and weaknesses. Use its strengths and bypass its weaknesses. If your message relies heavily on visual impact, don't try to convey it by radio. Words can never describe adequately what the eye can perceive with ease. Television is your preeminent visual medium. But television is stingy with its time. It has thousands of messages to deliver each day, with only 24 hours in the day and only four hours of prime time. If your message is too complex to fit into a 30-second spot or even into a 10-minute segment of a talk show, you may want to consider one of the print media. Remember too that television aims for the broad audience. If you want to reach a small audience with specific interests, a specialty publication may be your medium.

Radio stations do aim for specific audiences. Some target their programming toward youthful audiences, some toward the Baby Boomer generation. Different stations may aim for audiences at different educational and income levels. In some areas, you'll find stations that target different ethnic and linguistic groups. But complex messages rarely play well on radio. The average listener's attention span is relatively short.

General-circulation newspapers offer many vehicles for your message. You may submit a news release, pay for an advertisement, write a letter to the editor or submit a column for the editorial or commentary pages. Newspapers also can display photographs and drawings—often in color—though, of course, they can't match the visual impact of television. Most subscribers to general-circulation newspapers are over 30 years of age, and though different sections appeal to different groups, newspapers can't provide the pinpoint targeting of specialty publications. In considering a newspaper as a medium, take into consideration the newspaper's circulation: How many households does it reach? Where are these households?

Public speaking can be a powerful medium if properly used. Let's say that you're a developer who wants to build town houses adjacent to a single-family neighborhood. The people in the neighborhood are opposed. Your most effective approach may be a public presentation before a neighborhood audience in which you explain your project, using visuals, and answer questions from the audience.

Public speaking can also be the doorway to other media. If

you're invited to address a civic club or other group on a timely subject, ask the program chairman whether it will be all right to invite the media. If the media send reporters and cameras, your message may carry well beyond the walls of the meeting room.

MAKE MAXIMUM USE OF THE MEDIUM

Once you've chosen the medium, look for ways to make maximum use of it. Each medium has its distinctive characteristics. Learn them and use them to obtain the desired response.

Six tips will help you target your presentation for the desired response:

(1) *Be sensitive to the way your audience will experience the presentation.*

Put yourself in the shoes of the person who is receiving your message. How would you respond if the message came to you?

Each day, my desk is the target of a blizzard of paper. Some of it is important, some of it is trivial, and some of it is worthless. Separating the important stuff from the trivial stuff is time-consuming. I know that executive clients of mine experience the same problem, so I try to make it easier for them. I try to handle as many details as possible in person or by telephone. A telephone call can save time and eye strain, and it's easier on the landfill.

If I do have to communicate important matters on paper, I don't want my communication to get lost in the blizzard that descends on the recipient's desk. So I send it by a commercial air-express service. It costs more than regular mail, but it offers some significant advantages. I know that it will be handed to the client personally. The client will open the packet and find an attractive presentation and a request for immediate response. My communication will get priority over the other written materials that arrive. By being sensitive to the way my clients experience my presentation, I can tailor it for maximum impact. It works.

(2) *Don't overload your presentation.*

Sometimes we expect a presentation to accomplish too many things at once. You can't use a van simultaneously as a pick-up truck, a mini-bus and a camper. You have to choose the function you want it to serve.

Correspondingly, you can't use a brochure simultaneously to promote, explain, remind, build prestige and provide a source of exhaustive information. A brochure can handle any one of these functions, but not all of them at once. Concentrate on a few compatible functions for your presentation, and concentrate on these.

(3) *Make your presentation attractive.*

People judge you by the quality of your presentations. Go before an audience of business executives in an old, wrinkled, misfitting suit with your hair disheveled and your face showing a lack of acquaintance with a razor (if you're a man) or a make-up brush (if you're a woman). See how many people listen.

Send out a piece of printed matter with small, hard-to-read type jammed tightly onto pages of cheap paper and see how many people read it.

Market yourself with a videotape with faded, shaky, fuzzy images of you in a dull, nondescript office and see what kind of results you get.

A poor presentation is worse than no presentation at all. Going first class costs a few bucks more, but it pays dividends. If you're preparing a brochure or other written communication, invest in commercial art, color printing and enough paper to permit an attractive layout. If you can't afford the extra paper, cut back on the length of your copy, not on the quality of your presentation.

(4) *Develop a strong sense of timing.*

Before the days of round-the-clock television coverage, a major morning newspaper decided that its subscribers in the hinterlands would read the results of the national election in the next morning's edition, come hell or high water.

The presses were put on hold and a story was prepared so that all that was needed to make it complete was one paragraph: the opening paragraph telling who won.

The news came in, the story was completed and the presses rolled.

So did the train that carried the newspapers to the hinterlands. But it rolled minutes before the circulation truck arrived with its cargo of newspapers. Not only did the subscribers in the hinterlands miss the story about the election results; they also missed every other story carried in the paper that day.

Timing was the crucial factor.

Timing is a major factor in business communications as well. Direct-mail merchandisers have learned that the response to a mailing is heavily dependent on timing. If you're selling Christmas cards, you don't send out your catalog on December 10. If you're selling week-ends at Niagara Falls, you don't time your promotion for December. Holidays, seasons and even the days of the week on which your presentations arrive can have a profound effect on the response. So can the length of a presentation. If it takes too long to read a presentation, the recipient is likely to toss it before your message gets across.

(5) *Cultivate a sense of pacing to sustain interest.*

The attention span for most people is on the order of two or three minutes. Whether they're reading or listening, they'll switch mental channels unless there's a change of pace.

Notice the programming pattern on your favorite radio station. The average song will last about three minutes, unless you're listening to a classical work. The music companies know that's about the limit of the average listener's attention span. The tempo will change from one recording to another. A vocal selection will be followed by an instrumental; a pulsating rock beat by a mellow "oldie"; a lively Polonaise by a soothing sonata.

Professional speakers pace their points, using pauses, stories and audience exercises to sustain attention. And they know just when to conclude.

Pick up a novel and thumb through the pages. Which ones look more inviting? Probably the ones with lots of dialogue, because dialogue breaks up the paragraphs. Long paragraphs lend a gray, unbroken appearance to the page. Short paragraphs promise a constant change of pace. That's why newspaper writing is characterized by short paragraphs. Good writers use dialogue, similes, metaphors, analogies, subheadings and other devices to provide a constant variety of pace.

(6) *Stage every presentation to create the mood you want.*

Remember television's Jackie Gleason Show? It opened each week with an elaborate and colorful dance number by the June Taylor dancers. The dance and the music set the stage for the grand entrance of the flamboyant comedian.

On Broadway, the splashy opening number was a standard feature of musical productions until Richard Rodgers and Oscar Hammerstein II broke the mold. They had a lone cowboy ride slowly across the stage, with its quiet, pastoral backdrop. Out of the hush that filled the theater, the opening number rose like the voice of a lark breaking the morning silence, and the audience heard for the first time the haunting Hammerstein lyric perfectly attuned to the Rodgers music: *There's a bright golden haze on the meadow.*

Oh what a beautiful morning it was! *Oklahoma!* took off like a frisky colt, and musical history was made. The opening number set the perfect mood for the production that followed.

Staging gets the audience ready for your presentation. One of the most effective examples in my experience was General Electric's national sales convention in Honolulu's Sheraton Waikiki Resort Hotel. GE invited me to speak to the group.

The staging began well in advance of my presentation. These were GE's top sales people—the folks who put the power into the bottom line. Nothing was too good for them. Each time they went to their rooms, they would find a treat of some kind—some exotic food or interesting wine.

Months in advance, GE's planners had hired a musical group, which delivered announcements in songs it had composed. Everything was designed to set a positive, upbeat mood. When I stepped onto that stage to speak, the audience had been well prepared to hear what I had to say.

This generation has grown up with professionally staged presentations. It expects to be approached with flair and excitement. If you don't provide it, your audience will sense that something is lacking.

This is true all over the world. Graeme Clegg, my friend and client, owns a company based in Auckland, New Zealand, which sells products through direct distributors in more than a dozen countries in Asia, Australia and the Pacific Rim. You should see the meetings Graeme holds for his distributors. Each one is a major production, with music and dance numbers as part of the presentation. Even the decor is designed to capture the attention.

The art of presentation has become more sophisticated at the dawn of the 21st century. Newspapers and magazines once used screaming headlines to draw people into their presentations. Now they use creative layouts and graphic art, making liberal use of color.

Television uses colorful backdrops, technical legerdemain and mood-setting music to launch its presentations. Radio heralds its announcements with musical lead-ins. Direct-mail houses use sweepstakes, and stores use displays, lighting and other attention-getting devices to bring people in. Shopping malls compete to see which can provide the most exciting setting for shoppers to make their purchasing decisions. No matter what type of presentation you're making, set the stage with imagination and flair.

The time and resources spent on the message and the presentation would be wasted, of course, without a concrete purpose in mind. The object of your message is to obtain results. In the next chapter, we'll show how to focus on the results you want to achieve.

CHAPTER 17

Focusing Your Results

The object of a communication is to make things happen. If nothing happens, the communication fails. Often, we become so involved in making a superb speech, creating a literary gem or producing a smashing layout that we forget to ask ourselves: What results are we seeking?

We become like the surgeon who brilliantly opened the incision, excised the tumor without damaging surrounding organs and closed the wound cleanly and expertly, only to find a dead patient on the table. It was small consolation for the family that "the operation was a success, but the patient died."

THE MODEL A FIZZLED

The history of commerce is replete with comparable stories.

The Model A Ford is regarded today as one of the most memorable automobiles ever built. Like its sturdy predecessor, the Model T, it was tough and reliable. Unlike the homely "T," it had style and flair. It was a good performer for its day, and even after World War II it was still commonly used as a family car. It was a good car and a good-looking car. But it was not a successful car.

The Model A could not regain for Ford the sales lead that had been snatched from it by the upstart Chevrolet. The Model A lasted only four model years before it was replaced by the famous Ford V-8.

THE STEAMSHIP THAT SAILED TOO LATE

The SS *United States* was a beautiful ship—fast, luxurious and well-designed. It brought to the United States the world speed record for trans-Atlantic steamship crossings, beating earlier records set by Cunard Lines' Queen Mary and Queen Elizabeth. But it was launched at the dawn of the jet age, and soon the jumbo jets rendered it obsolete.

THE NUCLEAR SHIP THAT SAILED TOO SOON

The NS *Savannah,* was another beautiful ship, and a technological marvel in the bargain. It was the world's first nuclear powered merchant ship. As a design, it was eminently successful. But disputes with maritime unions over the manning of the vessel led to its early retirement.

AN INNOVATIVE FLOP

The Chevrolet Corvair was an innovative automobile, with a rear-mounted, air-cooled aluminum engine. It was comfortable, good-looking, economical and reasonably priced. But it could not compete for sales with the more conventional Ford Falcon, and Chevrolet eventually had to junk it in favor of the Chevy II, which evolved into the Nova.

In each of these cases, the operation was a success, but the patient died.

Why?

RESULTS ARE WHAT COUNTS

The efforts, though brilliantly executed, failed to produce the desired results.

In communications, we may spend a lot of time and talent crafting a superb message and delivering it in a compelling manner to an audience eager to receive it. But if we have given no thought to the *results* we're seeking, the audience won't respond in the way we want, and the message will fail. Results don't happen. They have to be programmed.

When an audience fails to respond to a message in the desired way, it's usually because the audience never knew what response was desired. And usually, the reason the desired response is unclear to the audience is that it's unclear to the communicator too.

So before you make your presentation, ask yourself: "What if the audience did exactly what I want it to do? What would that be, and how would I know it?"

TWO KINDS OF SUCCESS

Before you answer that question, think about the kinds of success you're seeking. There are two kinds, so far as communication is concerned. There is *short-range success* and there's *long-range success.*

When the audience lets you know that it enjoyed the presentation and understood the points you were making, you've achieved short-range success.

When the communication moves the audience to take the action you wanted it to take, you've achieved long-range success.

THE UNDERSTANDING DIDN'T GO FAR ENOUGH

Let me give you an example.

The investors in a franchise operation wanted to sell franchises in a certain part of the country. They knew the proposition was complex, so they invited prospects to regional meetings and carefully outlined the details. They used visual aids and handouts and held question-and-answer sessions.

The short-term results were excellent. After the first round of presentations, 80% of the people who attended said they would buy franchises. All who attended were given two weeks to respond.

At the end of the period, none of the prospects was on board. When the investors looked into the reasons, they learned why. The prospects who attended the meeting understood the proposal. But they were unable to explain it adequately to their spouses, lawyers and accountants. So in the long term, the investors' communication had failed.

The investors tried again. This time, they asked prospects to bring their spouses and at least one adviser. By explaining the proposition to each person involved in the decision-making, they achieved long-term success.

I have a client who never makes a hiring decision for an important position with his company without first interviewing the prospect's spouse. When the prospect says "yes" to the job offer, you have achieved short-term success. When the spouse is also sold on the job, the company and the location, then you are far more likely to achieve long-term success because you've increased the likelihood of a satisfactory, lasting relationship.

TWO KINDS OF FEEDBACK

To achieve both kinds of success, you need two kinds of feedback: *presentation feedback* and *message feedback.*

Presentation feedback tells you whether your audience heard and understood what you said. Message feedback tells you whether the audience responded the way you wanted it to respond.

The amount and type of feedback you seek depends upon your goals for making a presentation.

Let us say that you're launching an advertising campaign for your new line of personal computers. Since you're aiming for the household market, you've decided to use newspaper advertisements. What kind of feedback might you seek?

You might want to know which newspapers draw the best responses. You might want to know which wording is most effective, what day of the week is best to advertise, how frequently your ads should run and what size is most cost effective. All this is presentation feedback.

Advertising agencies have complex systems for obtaining this information. You can get it by including in the ads coupons with coded symbols that tell you which newspapers they were clipped from and the day of the week the ad was published. Or you can have responses directed to a post office box with code letters in the number to let you know which ad was being answered. Use your imagination to come up with other ways of obtaining the feedback.

Now let us suppose that you've just inaugurated a continuous quality-improvement process, and you've just explained it to your employees, perhaps through an article in your company publication, through a letter to employees, or through a speech.

Now you're not so much concerned about how well the presentation went over as you are with the level of understanding among your employees. How do you gauge it?

A simple questionnaire might do the job. If the questionaire shows that the program is well understood, you need only follow through with your implementation plans. If it shows that the employees are confused about certain aspects of the plan, you can devise additional communications addressing those specific areas.

EXPECT SURPRISES

When you seek feedback, expect surprises. It's been said that the Chevrolet Nova experienced sales resistance among Spanish-speaking people, not because the product lacked the qualities they were looking for, but because the expression "No va" in Spanish means "No go."

Don't look for the feedback that strokes your ego. And don't look for the kind that reinforces your biases. If feedback is going to help you, it has to come with the bark off. If the feedback is unfavorable, don't dismiss it as ignorant or unfair. Look for ways to change your presentation so that it yields positive feedback.

RECOGNIZING THE DESIRED RESPONSE

How will you know when the audience gives the response you desire?

The time to ask that question is *before* you go into your presentation. I've found it useful, early in the preparation stage, to write out a succinct statement specifying the response I desire, then planning the feedback that will tell me whether I've gained that response.

In some cases, you may find that the presentation you've planned just doesn't have the power to give you the desired response. If that's the case, you can do one of two things: You can plan another presentation that has the power you need. Or you can lower your expectations.

In other cases, you may spot some weak places in your presentation, and you can adjust to take care of the weaknesses.

STRATEGIES FOR OBTAINING FEEDBACK

Here are some time-tested strategies for obtaining feedback:

♦ *Test your presentation and message, not the audience.*

If the message isn't getting through, it's rarely the fault of the audience. Sure, some audiences are more savvy than others, and some are friendlier than others. But part of your challenge as a communicator is to know the audience you're facing and design your presentation to appeal to that audience.

If your feedback tells you that you didn't connect, find out why, and look for ways to make the connection the next time.

♦ *Test your effectiveness, not your abilities.*

Don't ask your audience, "Did you enjoy the presentation?" Few people are going to look you in the eye and say "You really bombed." Most people will tell you that you did fine. Some will heap glowing praise on you. That may be great for your ego, but it won't help you improve your presentation.

A local television talk-show host once opened a new series of shows and found that he was getting a new kind of feedback.

"When I was doing another show, people would come up to me and tell me they'd seen the show and enjoyed it," he said. "Now they stop me on the street to give me their opinions about the subjects we're discussing."

You can obtain this kind of feedback by asking specific questions about what you had to say. When people pay you compliments, draw them out with questions to determine whether they understand what you've said.

♦ *Ask your audience for feedback.*

If you're giving a speech, make it clear that you're not evaluating the audience, but that you're interested in its opinions.

"I've been telling you what I think; now I'd like to hear what you think about this subject," is a good way to introduce your request for feedback. On radio or television, you can ask your viewers or listeners to respond by telephone or letter. If you're running an ad in a print medium, a brief invitation to respond or a brief questionnaire that can be clipped and mailed can elicit feedback. Coupons accompanying an ad can tell you how many customers are responding to a specific message.

♦ *Devise a way of evaluating the feedback you get.*

Direct mailers know from experience how many responses they should receive from their mailers. When there's a money-back guarantee, they set an acceptable quota for returned merchandise. When they get more responses and fewer returns than they expect, they know they've been successful. If the responses are too low and the returns too high, they know to make adjustments.

♦ *Tailor your feedback and evaluations to your ultimate goals.*

Let's say you have a product that is popular with the Baby Boomers, and you want to extend its appeal to the younger generation. So you develop an advertising campaign aimed at the younger generation. Your feedback from the younger consumers is favorable. They're turning on to your product. But remember your ultimate goal. It isn't to sell your product to young consumers. It's to *broaden* its appeal so that it will appeal to all age groups. So while you're congratulating yourself on your success with younger consumers, you might want to see how your advertising message is affecting your older customers. If it's turning them off, then some adjustments need to be made.

FEEDBACK IS USELESS UNLESS USED

Feedback is useless unless it's used, and there are a number of ways to use it.

If your feedback indicates that your presentation was a resounding success, there's a tendency to sit back and bask in the accolades. But remember that a successful presentation is not an end in itself. You're looking for long-term results. Your presentation may have resulted in brilliant solutions to long-term problems, but devising solutions isn't enough. You have to implement them. What long-range response were you seeking? While the short-term response is ringing in your ears, get busy taking the steps that will ensure the long-term achievement.

USE FAILURES TO BUILD SUCCESS

If your feedback is negative, don't go away depressed. Use your failures to build toward future successes. Analyze what went wrong and look for ways to prevent it from happening again. Negative feedback can be your key to constant improvement.

Good communicators use their experiences to learn what works best for them. The self-effacing style of Wendy's founder Dave Thomas wouldn't work for hard-charging GE executive Jack Welch. Actor Eddie Murphy's racy street-flavored humor wouldn't work for the suave Johnny Carson. My style might not work for you. The important thing is to develop your own style and learn what works best for you. I listen and analyze my feedback so that I can fine-tune every presentation for maximum effectiveness.

KEEP THE INITIATIVE IN YOUR HANDS

Some people believe their feedback has been successful when members of the audience ask for their business cards. I'd rather not give them my card. I prefer that they give me their cards. That way, the initiative remains in my hands.

When I'm asked for my card, I usually ask, "Was there something in particular that interested you?" If the answer is "Yes," I find out what it was. Then I say, "I'm often hard to reach by telephone. Give me your business card and I'll see that you get the information you want." On the back of the card, I'll note what the person was interested in. Then I'll make sure the information is provided. Later I'll call to see whether the individual was satisfied. This personal attention often opens doors for future opportunities. It's easier to get through to busy people when you're giving them information they've requested than it is to reopen a door they've closed.

As you learn to focus your communication efforts, you'll find yourself growing in effectiveness as a leader of people and an influencer of events. People will not only receive your message; they will also understand it and act on it.

In the remaining portions of the book, we will be examining some specific avenues of communication. The public platform is a powerful forum for influencing groups, and it offers you a chance to be heard far beyond the walls of the room where you speak. In Part Four, I'll pass along some suggestions that have served me well during my career as a public speaker. We'll begin, in Chapter Eighteen, by looking at ways to prepare an effective speech.

PART FOUR

Platform Power

CHAPTER

18

Preparing for Your Speech

With all the technological wonders of the 21st century, business executives will still find one of their most effective communications media to be the one employed with such skill by Demosthenes 2,300 years ago: the art of public speaking.

For reaching a widely dispersed audience quickly and economically, telecommunications will be indispensable. But telecommunications media cannot present the message in the flesh. They can't put communicator and audience in a shared ambience. Only the live public speech can do that, and nothing can stir the emotions like a live speech, eloquently crafted and superbly delivered.

OCCASIONS FOR PUBLIC SPEAKING

A public speech can be used to communicate a corporate vision to the employees. It can be used to guide employee motivation in the direction an executive wants it to go. It can be used to create favorable images of the company and the executive in the community. It can be used to persuade public bodies to take action in harmony with the company's best interests. A public speech can exhort, entertain, explain and persuade. While it reaches only a limited immediate audience, its secondary audiences can be immense. People go back to their homes and offices and tell others what they've heard. The media may listen and publish excerpts from the speech and the gist of what was said. Television and radio stations may extract sound bites.

So the art of public speaking is well worth cultivating, and the preparation for a public speech deserves careful attention.

THREE TYPES OF SPEECH

The type of preparation you undertake will depend upon the type of speech you give. There are three basic types of public speech:

(1) *Impromptu.*
(2) *Written text.*
(3) *Extemporaneous.*

IMPROMPTU SPEECHES

The impromptu speech usually is the most intimidating for the speaker, though it need not be. This is the speech you have to give on the spur of the moment, without benefit of notes or outline.

It may happen when you're recognized from the platform at a public function and you're called upon for "a few appropriate remarks."

It may happen at a board meeting when you're unexpectedly called upon to explain a project you're in charge of or a proposal you've made.

Or it may happen when you're the program chairman for a service club meeting and the scheduled speaker fails to show.

Stay Calm

Two words are important to keep in mind under such circumstances: ***Don't panic.***

If you're frequently called upon to speak in behalf of your company, it pays to keep a "generic speech" on hand. This speech might contain your core message: the essence of what you want people to know about your organization. It should contain information that you're familiar with and don't have to look up. If you can't keep a copy of this speech in your briefcase, at least be familiar with its general outline, so that when you are called upon unexpectedly you can quickly organize your thoughts.

When the call comes, take a moment to think. Make a quick mental outline of the points you want to make. Don't worry about the words you'll use. Just organize the ideas. The words will come, just as the words come to you when you're engaged in ordinary conversation.

WRITTEN TEXTS

A young minister once asked his outspoken grandmother for a critique of his first sermon.

"I saw only three things wrong with it," she said, to her grandson's relief.

"What three things were wrong?" he asked. Her answer dispelled his relief:

"First, you read it. Second, you didn't read it well. Third, it wasn't worth reading."

If you can help it, don't read from a text. Unless you're an excellent reader, and something of an actor, it will sound stiff and unnatural.

However, there are occasions when it's necessary to read a speech. When it's critically important that the information be delivered precisely and accurately, reading may be your only choice. If you're dealing with touchy legal issues, for instance, one stray *ad lib* might cost you dearly.

The procedure for developing and organizing a written text is similar to that for an extemporaneous speech, which I'll deal with in detail a little later. In an extemporaneous speech, you organize your ideas. In a written speech, you go one step farther and put the ideas into the actual words you'll be speaking.

As you write, remember that written language has one style and spoken language another. Write for the spoken language. Express your thoughts the way you would express them in a conversation, not the way you would write them in a letter or essay. Remember, too, that the eye can glide over words that stumble the tongue. Read the text aloud and make sure there are no tongue-twisters and no difficult-to-pronounce combinations.

When delivering the speech, don't read word for word. Let your eye take in clusters of words, so that your mind is dealing with *ideas,* not syllables. This will make it easier for you to express the ideas naturally and fluently.

A smooth, natural delivery will be easier if you are thoroughly familiar with the text. Don't try to memorize it, but know how it's organized and know what points you want to stress. You may want to underline the words you wish to emphasize and note the places you want to pause.

Thorough familiarity with the text will enable you to look up to maintain eye contact with the audience without fear of losing your place. If you do lose your place, don't worry. Calmly scan the page until you come to the right line. It will take only a moment, and you won't lose your audience.

EXTEMPORANEOUS SPEECHES

Extemporaneous speeches are usually the most effective. When speaking extemporaneously, you are guided by a carefully prepared outline, but you're not tied to a specific text. Your outline provides you with the ideas you want to express. You can then form these ideas into words in your natural, conversational way. This type of speech combines the advantages of spontaneity and good organization.

Since the majority of experienced speakers use the extemporaneous approach, most of the material that follows will deal with preparing an extemporaneous speech. However, most of the suggestions are equally applicable to the written text.

SHOULD YOU ACCEPT?

A good speech demands careful and creative preparation. The preparation begins before you decide to accept the invitation to speak. Your decision should be guided by the answers to these questions:

(1) Why should I speak to this audience in this place at this time?
(2) What should I speak about?
(3) How can I make it enjoyable, interesting, informative and persuasive?
(4) How should I organize my speech?
(5) How can I prepare myself to make a good delivery?
(6) How can I keep calm and avoid stage fright during my speech?
(7) How can I connect with my listeners and keep them involved?
(8) What barriers to communication might I experience and how can I deal effectively with them?
(9) How can I clarify complex ideas, be convincing on controversial claims, and inject interest in otherwise dull material?
(10) How will I get the response I want from my audience, and how will I know when I get it?

WHY YOU AND WHY NOW

The importance of Question one should be obvious. If you have nothing to say that will be useful or interesting to this group, then you shouldn't speak. If you are scheduled at a time and place and in a context that will make it difficult if not impossible for you to deliver your message effectively, then you should decline the invitation.

Before you accept, learn as much as you can about the organization that extends the invitation. Know its background, history and purpose. If you accept the invitation to speak, will others interpret your acceptance as an endorsement of its goals? If so, are they goals you can comfortably endorse?

Find out about the interests of the people you're invited to address. What do they already know about the things you speak on? What can you tell them that will add to their useful knowledge? How much time will you have in which to tell them?

Who else is on the program and what are their topics? In what order will they speak? How will your speech and your message fit into the overall program? Will you follow a dynamic or a boring speaker? Will the speech preceding yours by informative or inspirational?

IDENTIFY THE BARRIERS

Identify the barriers you may have to overcome to put your message across. Will this be a sympathetic, a hostile or a neutral audience? Are you opening the program? Are you closing it? What kind of room arrangements will you find? Will you be the last speaker before lunch or the first after lunch? Will your audience come to you directly from a cocktail hour?

All these considerations are important in deciding whether this speech is likely to advance or retard your purpose. Don't go into a situation in which you know it will be hard to look good. If the deck seems stacked against you, pass.

REASONS TO ACCEPT

But with most invitations, you'll probably find plenty of good reasons to accept. Here are some good reasons for saying yes:

♦ You have some valuable information or insights you want to give to the group.
♦ Now is an appropriate time, and this is an appropriate place to share them.
♦ This audience will accept your leadership, provided you earn it when you speak.
♦ You have something important you want this audience to do.

CHOOSING A TOPIC

Once you've decided to accept the invitation, your next task is to choose your topic. Here are some criteria for selecting a topic:

♦ It should be something you know about or can find out about.
♦ It should be a subject the audience knows at least a little about but wants to know more about.
♦ It should be timely and appropriate for the audience.
♦ It should be narrow enough that it won't be confusing.
♦ It should be instrumental in achieving the response you want.

GATHER YOUR MATERIALS

After you've chosen your topic, analyze what you already know about it and decide how much additional information you'll need. You're now ready to research your speech.

Use the library, periodicals, your own files and any other appropriate resources to fill in the gaps in your knowledge of the subject. Then, to make it truly your own speech, draw upon your personal experiences to provide vivid illustrations or use your imagination to produce original stories.

ORGANIZING YOUR SPEECH

A lot of complicated formulas have been advanced for organizing speeches and other communications. It doesn't have to be complicated. It can be a simple matter of choosing the material you want to use and following your mind's natural selection process. Here's how I do it:

(1) I go through all my material and select only those points that are relevant to my audience and my speech.

(2) I write out one concise sentence that clearly tells what I'm going to say.

(3) I reduce my ideas to three or four sentences that clearly present the idea expressed in my topic sentence. I arrange them in the most convincing order. This becomes my outline.

(4) I flesh out the outline with explanations, supportive statements, funny lines and stories, and persuasive points.

(5) I select a humorous related story to use in my introduction and a brief summation of main points to use as my conclusion. I will end my speech with a clear, convincing challenge for specific action.

(6) I let it ripen in my mind and heart until I understand the implications of everything I will say, feel it very deeply, and am sure every point is as clear and convincing as I can make it.

Now I'm ready to deliver the speech in words that are spontaneous, but that spring from well-organized, deeply felt thoughts.

WHEN YOU USE A SPEECH WRITER

Speech writing is a communication specialty in itself. It is also time-consuming. Not all executives have the time or the inclination to devote to the craft. That's why corporations often have a staff of speech writers, or delegate the task to members of their public-relations departments.

This works fine, so long as the speech writer knows the executive's thoughts and speech patterns. If the speech writer doesn't know you well, you could find yourself looking at a speech that distorts your viewpoint and uses a style of expression that is not natural for you.

The better the speech writers know you, the better they can express your ideas in your kind of language. If the speech writers don't report directly to you, they should report to someone who knows you very well, and that person should edit the draft very carefully.

Make sure the writing staff has a clear understanding of your position on the issues you plan to address. If you have company literature or correspondence that states the official position, make it available to your writer. Your writing staff should have a library of corporate literature, including annual reports, sales and marketing literature, external and internal publications, and a file of executive speeches. When you come across articles or quotations that you find especially relevant or cogent, have your secretary clip them or copy them and send them to the writing staff.

It will help the writer to have samples of your speaking or writing on hand. This can take the form of audiotapes, videotapes, speech manuscripts and copies of correspondence. Such resources will enable the writers to familiarize themselves with your speech patterns and your word choices.

If you have trouble pronouncing certain words or word combinations, the writer should know about it.

A competent writer will provide you with a well-organized and well-written script. Your task is to personalize it.

Never go to the platform with a speech you haven't read before. Take the time to read the draft while you are not rushed and are not distracted.

Read the speech first for content. Has the writer included all the points you want to make? Is all the information factual? Does it express the viewpoint you want to express? Does it reflect your priorities?

Next read it for style. Does the writer use any words that are unfamiliar to you? objectionable to you? incompatible with your style of expression?

Next read the speech aloud. Do the words flow smoothly and naturally from your lips? Are there any tongue-twisters? Are there any sentences that you can't speak in a single breath?

Don't hesitate to second-guess your writer on the wording. This is *your* speech and it should say what you want to say the way you want to say it. Make any word changes you think are necessary to make it conform to your natural form of expression.

As you read it, be alert for opportunities to add personal stories and anecdotes that will put your imprint on the speech. Stories and images can add life, interest and inspiration to your speech. In the next chapter, we'll provide suggestions on finding and choosing these elements.

chapter 19

Communicating Through Images and Stories

If communication were just a matter of passing along information and ideas, speakers could save their breaths. All they'd need to do would be to pass out copies of their outlines. But when people come to hear speeches, they're looking for more than raw information. They expect to be entertained or inspired as well as informed and persuaded. Information and ideas must be passed along with a skillful leavening of humor, pathos, and captivating illustrations.

That's why experienced speakers have learned to employ images and stories to bring their speeches to life. Stories and images enable them to make their speeches enjoyable, interesting, informative and persuasive.

CHOOSE YOUR STORIES

Storytelling is an art, but you can learn it. The first thing you have to learn is how to choose your stories. Select each story with these criteria in mind:

♦ *It should be a story the audience can relate to.*

245

Probably the most effective storyteller of all time was Jesus of Nazareth, whose parables still make their points nearly 2,000 years after they were first uttered. The stories He told revolved around the everyday lives of the people in His audience.

When He told the parable of the lost sheep, He knew He was addressing an audience familiar with the routine of the shepherd. When He told the parable of the Good Samaritan, He knew that His audience had grown up in an environment of animosity between Jews and Samaritans, and would grasp the moral significance of a Samaritan man's stopping to render aid to a Jewish stranger. When He spoke about dough and leaven, He knew that in His audience were women who made bread by mixing sour dough with fresh dough for leavening, confident that "a little leaven ferments the whole lump."

When you use stories, follow His example. Make them stories people in your audience will be able to connect with through their common experiences.

And make sure they will relate to each story in a positive way. Once I was invited to address the annual sales meeting of Borden's, Inc., in Houston. I immediately began to think about all the stories I'd heard about Elsie the Cow. But, following my usual practice, I checked with someone at Borden's to find out whether it would be appropriate to joke about Elsie.

"Heaven's no," replied my contact. "We consider Elsie almost sacred."

♦ *The story must be clear and able to stand on its own.*

There's a truism about jokes and anecdotes: If you have to explain them, don't bother. If the audience doesn't immediately grasp the moral or the punchline, the story has bombed and no amount of explaining will rescue it. Sometimes a story may resonate among people who share your specific knowledge and expertise, but will fall flat among those who are not initiated. Avoid stories that require special knowledge or special vocabulary unless you know that your audience has that special knowledge and is familiar with the vocabulary.

If I say "a jumbo shrimp is an oxymoron," the line will fall flat with an audience that doesn't know that an oxymoron is a contradiction in terms, like a square circle or a straight curve.

Before I use a story with an audience, I practice telling it to several different people. By observing their responses, I can tell which stories click and which ones flop.

♦ *It must relate clearly to the point you wish to make.*

It isn't enough that a story be funny or poignant or captivating. It must also contribute toward the purpose of your speech. Its relationship to your message should be clear immediately. The audience should have no trouble figuring out how the story relates to the point you're making.

Some speakers like to start out with a joke: "A funny thing happened to me on the way to the hotel . . . ." They tell it, wait for the laughter to die, then say, "But seriously, though . . . ."

The joke has added nothing to the speech. Instead of leading the audience compellingly into the subject of your talk, it has flashed the message: "You've had your dessert. Now it's time to eat your spinach." The good part is over; the dull part begins. That's no way to capture and hold an audience.

♦ *The story must be one you can tell well.*

You may have heard the story about the new prison inmate who was puzzled by what happened after the lights went out. Someone called out a number, and suddenly the whole cellblock erupted in laughter. As the laughter died, someone called out another number, and again the inmates roared.

"What's going on?" the newcomer asked his cellmate.

"We're telling jokes," came the reply. "We don't hear many new ones on the inside, so we end up telling the same ones over and over.

Everybody knows them all, so to save time we've just numbered them. When I call out "Number 76," everybody knows which joke I'm talking about, so everybody laughs."

The new inmate wanted in on the fun, so he called out "Number 76." He was greeted by dead silence.

"Why didn't they laugh?" he asked.

"Some people can tell 'em and some can't," replied the cellmate.

It's true. A joke that goes over big when told by one speaker will be a dud when told by another. That's because the personality and background of the teller imparts a certain flavor to the joke. My buddy Robert Henry can tell jokes about Southern Baptists and get away with it, because he springs from Southern Baptist soil and the aura clings to him. A Jewish comedian can crack semitic jokes that would be offensive coming from a non-Jew. A black comedian can crack jokes that might be considered racist coming from a caucasian. A joke that works for a fast-talking gregarious personality might bomb when used by a more subtle, low-key personality. A story must be suited to the personality of the teller and must fit in with the mood of the speech.

♦ *The story must fit into the allotted time.*

Sometimes, when you're building toward a major point, a story can be stretched to obtain full impact. If you're making a minor point, you'll want to make it short and sweet. Be sure the length of the story is appropriate for the point you're making, and appropriate for the length of your speech.

PRACTICE TELLING YOUR STORY

If a story is worth telling, it's worth telling well. The only way you can be sure you're telling a story well is to practice it repeatedly.

A good story has rhythm and flow, and it has a mood. The only way you can give a story these qualities is to make it a part of you.

Tell the story over and over. Listen to yourself telling it on audiotape. Better yet, *watch* yourself telling it on videotape. Look for ways you can improve the way you tell it.

Many speakers spend hours rehearsing their main points and neglect to practice the storytelling. That's a mistake.

LET THE AUDIENCE RESPOND

If a story is to be effective, the audience must have a chance to respond to it. Use pauses to build anticipation for your punch line. After you've delivered your punchline, pause again to give the point a chance to sink in.

INVOLVE THE AUDIENCE

A good speech achieves interaction between the speaker and the audience. A good speaker looks for ways to involve the audience. A good story provides an avenue.

As I tell a story, I often ask questions that keep the audience responding. I'll reach a key point in the story line and will ask something like, "What do you think he did next?" If the audience is really with me, the answer will immediately pop into their minds, and I can tell, just by watching them, that I've connected.

The best way to involve the audience in funny stories is to tell the stories as if they were about people in the audience. If the people you choose are well known to the group, the results can be hilarious. It works on the same principle as the celebrity "roast." You may pick on a top executive, or a member of the group who is known as a cut-up, or a highly respected person in the audience.

There are four important rules for using the technique properly:

♦ Always make sure you clear it with the individual who will be the subject of your humor, or at least with someone who

249

knows the individual well enough to tell you whether the person may be offended.

♦ Keep it good-natured. Always make sure that your punchline doesn't land in a sensitive spot. Bob Hope liked to poke fun at Gerald Ford during Ford's presidency. But he always ribbed the president about his golf game, never about his foreign policy.

Most audiences will resent it if an outsider is perceived as attacking one of their group. My colleague, Gene Perret, who once served as head writer for Hope and Carol Burnett, remembers ruefully a speech he gave at a company function. He devoted an entire routine to making fun of a blueprint machine that never worked. In the middle of his speech, the manager of the department that made the machine walked out angrily.[1]

♦ Keep it short. If you run on and on about the same individual, people tend to get bored and the individual involved may be embarrassed.

♦ At the end, thank the person, either explicitly, by shaking hands, or by conveying a compliment.

ILLUMINATE WITH IMAGES

In Chapter Two, we learned that one of the keys to the Kingdom of Communication is the use of images. Images can illuminate your stories and your arguments.

Before you can use images, you must be able to see them—first with your literal eyes and secondly with your mental eyes.

You can't describe something you haven't seen, and you haven't really seen something until you've examined it carefully. Therefore, a good communicator must be a keen observer.

The poet Robert Frost was a meticulous observer.

"The Vermont mountains stretch extended straight," he wrote. "New Hampshire mountains curl up in a coil."

Who but a person intimately acquainted with the New England landscape could have written that description?

"Like a piece of ice on a hot stove, the poem must ride on its own melting," he wrote in a preface to his collected poems.

Frost had not only seen ice melting on a hot stove; he had keenly observed it.

When you're watching a movie or a television show, notice how the cameras pan the scene for a general view, then focus in on the specific thing the director wants you to notice.

Many of us go through life panning the landscape. We get a general view of our surroundings, but we seldom look at things up close. Those who do are rewarded with glimpses of uncommon beauty in little things.

The American Indian, before surrendering to the Europeanization of the continent, was a keen observer, because life and livelihood depended on close observation. Crowfoot, the Blackfoot warrior and orator, used poignant imagery derived from close observation in his memorable last words:

> *What is life? It is the flash of a firefly in the night. It is the breath of a buffalo in the wintertime. It is the little shadow which runs across the grass and loses itself in the sunset.*

That's imagery employed by someone who looked at his world closely and saw its vivid details.

If you take a keen interest in the little things happening around you, you'll find a wealth of images to employ in your communication.

After you've seen the image, your next challenge is to convey it to your audience in words that will accurately describe what you mean. This can get tricky, because members of the audience must fit the image into the pattern of their own individual experiences.

The possibility of misunderstanding is multiplied if your audience happens to come from a cultural or linguistic background different from the one you're familiar with. When Soviet leader Nikita Khrushchev visited the United States during the '50s, he used a bit of imagery that got hyped in the translation. Americans read that the flamboyant communist had boasted, "We will bury you." What Khrushchev had said—and what his Russian hearers understood him to say—was "We will surpass you."

Before you use imagery with a group, ask yourself two questions:

(1) *How might this audience misinterpret my imagery?*
(2) *What can I do to prevent misunderstanding?*

Images, like stories, must be chosen carefully with your audience and your message in mind. Here are some criteria to use in choosing images:

♦ *They should be clear and understandable to your audience.*

An acquaintance of mine who grew up on a Southern farm that lacked modern conveniences was once trying to describe a romantic scene to a young woman who was a generation younger and had grown up in a middle-class urban setting.

"The moon," he told her, "was big as a wash tub."

To him, the image was clear. But the young lady looked puzzled. "How big is a wash tub?" she asked.

♦ *They should be images that your audience can identify with.*

Your images should resonate among the day-to-day experiences of the audience.

An old textile mill hand once announced to his workmates, "My son just doffed off a set of twins."

To anyone unacquainted with textile-mill lingo, the announcement would be almost incomprehensible. But textile workers were familiar with the image of a "doffer" working his way up and down

252

the rows of spinning frames, rapidly snatching the full bobbins of yarn from the spindles, tossing them into a box, and replacing them with empty bobbins. He was "doffing off" the bobbins from the spindles. The old hand was announcing that his son had become the father of twins.

A farmer might have said, "My son just harvested a set of twins."

A salesperson might have said, "My son just closed on a set of twins."

Use your imagination, and your knowledge of the audience, to produce images that illuminate.

The classic example of failure to identify with an audience involved Marie Antoinette, wife of King Louis XVI of France. When told that the poor people of Paris were angry because they had no bread, she responded, "Let them eat cake."

The lady, born to royalty, could not identify with people whose options were bread or starvation, not bread or cake.

◆ *They should be useful.*

The image you use should accomplish a purpose in relation to your speech. Imagery used just for the sake of being cute serves no purpose.

In 1946, an invisible line running from the Baltic Sea to the Adriatic Sea separated the communist world from the free world. Winston Churchill gave it a name that captured its significance and fixed its image in the minds of the world. He called it the Iron Curtain. The term became a highly useful shorthand for the boundary between two conflicting ideologies.

Imagery can be used to inspire. When General Bernard E. Bee of South Carolina saw his troops about to buckle before the Union onslaught in the First Battle of Manassas, he pointed toward General Thomas Jackson of Virginia.

"Look at Jackson" he cried. "There he stands like a stone wall. Rally behind the Virginians!"

General Jackson was forever immortalized as Stonewall Jackson, and the name provided inspiration for the men who served under him.

Imagery can also be used to explain complex ideas by likening them to something the audience is familiar with. One writer, explaining the workings of a nuclear reactor, likened the nucleus of an atom to a rack of balls on a billiards table, ready to fly apart when struck by a speeding cueball.

♦ *Images should be vivid.*

William Shakespeare was a master of imagery:

"O tiger's heart wrapped in a woman's hide." **(King Henry VI.)**

"These words are razors to my wounded heart." **(Titus Andronicus.)**

"She hangs upon the cheek of night like a rich jewel in an Ethiop's ear." **(Romeo and Juliet).**

"He doth bestride the narrow world like a Colossus. . . ." **(Julius Caesar).**

Choose the images that vividly call attention to your message or its meaning.

♦ *Images should be concise.*

Think of the commercial images that sell: "Reach out and touch someone" (AT&T), "Like a rock" (Chevrolet trucks), "The best part of waking up" (Folgers Coffee).

♦ *Images should be memorable.*

Memorable images are not only vivid; they capture the essence of the message like a fine camera capturing the essence of a moment.

John McCrae immortalized the fallen American soldiers sleeping in a Belgian graveyard with this simple, vivid and memorable imagery:

In Flanders fields the poppies blow
Between the crosses, row on row

Recall, too, the memorable words of astronaut Neil Armstrong as he stepped from his lunar module and planted the first human footprints on the moon: "That's one small step for a man, one giant leap for mankind."

Think of the vivid image Dr. Martin Luther King Jr. used in his "I have a dream" speech: ". . . Little black children and little white children playing together on the red hills of Georgia."

These images are easily visualized. They capture the spirit of the message. They leave in the minds of the audience mental pictures that will help them remember the messages they adorn.

Images painted with words must be interpreted by the audience. If the audience doesn't "see" the same image that you see, the imagery goes for naught.

You can help your audience with the interpretation through four devices: ***repetition, reinforcement, feedback*** and ***application.***

Repetition

You may have been taught in school that good speakers never repeat themselves because repetition bores audiences.

I've found the opposite to be true. Generally, the people in your audience will appreciate the restatement of images because it helps them to fix the images in their minds. The key is to repeat the ideas, but to frame them and state them differently. This is a powerful aid to learning.

The experts tell us that more than two-thirds of what we hear vanishes from our minds after 24 hours. The percentage of information that sticks goes up markedly, however, when we hear it repeated several times.

You can use several different devices for repetition.

One is to *restate or review what you have just said.* Begin with the phrase, "In other words . . . ." The audience will know you're about to repeat the image in another way. The repetition will either help people focus on the image more clearly or to fix it more firmly in their minds.

You can *summarize what you've said by repeating significant points.* If the people in the audience remember the main points, they will find it easier to recall the details.

You can *interpret what you've said.* "Just as a cueball sends a rack of billiards balls flying in all directions, so a stray neutron from one atom of uranium can send the protons and neutrons of another atom flying apart."

You can *call attention to special things that should be remembered.* This is done by restating what you've already said: "Remember what I said earlier: A reactor in a nuclear power plant is just another device for boiling water. . . ."

Reinforcement

Reinforcement can come in visual or verbal form, and it can be presented as images or as supporting data.

You can provide *visual reinforcement* through slides or transparencies, through objects the audience can examine, or through images on handout sheets. Charts and graphs help people to visualize statistical information. Diagrams help them understand how things are put together, how devices work, and how things are laid out.

You give *verbal reinforcement* by painting other word pictures that emphasize the image you wish to convey. For example, during a talk I often say, "Now when I told that to an audience in [another city] they . . . ." Then I recreate the image as I described it to the other audience and describe their reaction to it.

Supportive data provide raw facts that reinforce the message conveyed by the image.

"If the pipes produced by this plant in a year's time were laid end to end, they would form a pipeline stretching from New York to San Francisco," you might say, displaying a map of the United States with a drawing of a pipeline stretching from coast to coast.

Then you could provide the supporting figures, listing the number of feet of each category of pipe the plant produced.

Feedback

Feedback lets you know whether the audience has understood your image the way you intended for it to be understood. The question should not be "Do you understand what I said?" The proper question is "What did you understand me to say?"

So if you're explaining how a nuclear power plant works, lead your audience through the process with questions designed to determine whether they understood your imagery:

"So if the nucleus of the atom is a rack of billiard balls, what do we call the cueball that comes flying into the rack?

"A neutron! You got it.

"And what happens when the neutron hits the nucleus?

"Right! The nucleus flies apart and produces energy. Now what do we use that energy to do?

"Boil water and make steam. So now you know how a nuclear plant works."

Don't be surprised if the audience sometimes misses the point. That's the value of feedback. It lets you know when your audience has received the wrong image, and gives you the opportunity to go back and set the picture straight.

Application

Perhaps the most effective method of assisting an audience in understanding your image is to make them participants in its application.

Once a speaker was cautioning his audience against compromising its stand against nudity and violence in movies. Many times, he said, it's tempting to say "This movie is all right; it only has one or two questionable scenes in it."

To dramatize his point, he held up a glass of clear water. This water, he said, had been taken from a pure mountain spring. He took a drink to demonstrate its purity.

Then he held up another glass, this one filled with a dirty-looking liquid.

"This water," he said, "was taken from a puddle in a pig sty."

His listeners crinkled their noses.

Then the speaker used an eye dropper to extract some of the filthy water from its glass. He put two drops into the glass of clean water and stirred it until there was no visible trace of the filth.

"Now," he said, passing the glass among his audience, "who would like a drink from this glass."

It was a point the audience would not forget. The speaker had drawn his listeners into the experience. The application was made unmistakably clear.

FINDING THE RIGHT IMAGE

At first, you may find it hard to come up with stories and images to illustrate the points you make. But keep your eyes open. As you read, make note of stories and illustrations that may be applicable to the things you want to say. Listen to the stories and images others use. Borrow shamelessly. Do you think John F. Kennedy or his speech writer, Theodore Sorensen, came up with the expression, "Ask not what your country can do for you; ask what you can do for your country"? Oliver Wendell Holmes Jr. used very similar words in an address to Union army veterans in 1884.

Do you think Franklin Roosevelt originated the expression, "The only thing we have to fear is fear itself"? A century earlier, the Duke of Wellington said "The only thing I am afraid of is fear." More than

200 years before Wellington, Francis Bacon wrote, "Nothing is terrible except fear itself."

So listen, read, borrow and adapt—always acknowledging the source of the material you've borrowed (it's both unethical and illegal to plagiarize the work of others).

Be a keen observer of the ideas, events and scenes that make up your world, and let your communication sparkle with reflections of the things you've seen, heard and experienced. You'll find your speeches taking on new life.

Your speech gains its ultimate effectiveness when you are at one with your audience: when your listeners follow your every word, thought and movement willingly and effortlessly. You can achieve this kind of oneness with your audience if you practice the suggestions in the next chapter.

20

Captivating Your Audience

Perhaps you have watched with envy as a skillful speaker strode confidently to the platform and immediately played the audience like a fine instrument.

Such performances don't just happen. They're the results of careful planning. You can achieve the same kind of effect if you follow the right strategies. Let's look at four effective strategies:

BE SENSITIVE TO YOUR AUDIENCE

You may have heard of the tough sergeant who was told to break the news gently to Pvt. Jackson that the recruit's mother had died. The sergeant called his unit together and told them: "I want all you guys whose mothers are still alive to take one step forward." And as most of the recruits stepped forward, the sergeant quickly added: "Not so fast, Jackson."

A lot of speakers are just that insensitive when they communicate with their audiences. They deliver the message without worrying about how their hearers might receive it. Such speakers have a hard time establishing rapport with an audience.

Skilled communicators try to understand their audiences. They want to know what their listeners think and feel, and they design their presentations to appeal to the particular audience they're addressing.

This doesn't mean that they try to tell the audience what the audience wants to know. There was no way Private Jackson could welcome the news that his mother had died. But there was a way that the sergeant might have approached him gently and paved the way for the unsettling news.

Good speakers work to establish common ground with their audiences, even when they know an audience may disagree with some of the things they have to say. That common ground is vital, even with friendly audiences. Audiences are always more receptive to speakers who demonstrate respect for their attitudes and thoughts.

The Christian apostle Paul demonstrated an ability to establish common ground when he addressed an audience of polytheistic Greeks on Mars Hill in Athens. How was he going to persuade them to look into a religion that worshiped only one God, and an unseen one at that?

Paul began by calling attention to all the gods to which the Greeks had erected altars. Then he noted that one altar was dedicated to an "unknown god." This unknown, unseen God was the one he wanted to tell them about.

The good speaker plays the role of the host. It's no accident that the master of ceremonies on a television show is identified as "your host." The job of a host is to anticipate people's wants and needs, to take care of them, and to make people feel comfortable and at home.

That's the job of a good speaker, too. The pros remember the purposes behind their presentations, but they also look for ways to make the audience feel comfortable and unthreatened.

It's a poor speaker who comes before an audience behaving like a guest—as if it's up to the audience to adjust to the speaker's wave length. It's up to you to adjust your wave length to the audience.

Like a good host, a good speaker will respect the audience's comfort zone. Let me illustrate. Have you ever gone into a store to buy a specific product and had the salesperson pounce like a lion rising to the prey? It makes you want to turn around and look for the same item in another store, doesn't it? You know that the salesperson has one thing in mind: making that sale. Your wants and needs are secondary considerations, if they're considered at all. You're wary, because even though the salesperson can sell you what you want and need, you're not sure that your best interests are going to be served. Your comfort zone has been violated. Your confidence in the salesperson has been diminished.

You'll respond favorably, though, to the salesperson who approaches with a friendly smile, takes the time to find out what you need, then looks for ways to help you fill your needs.

It's the same with a speaker. Audiences have their comfort zones, which they tend to protect from intruders. And they regard as intruders those speakers who come on too fast and too strong, more intent on proving themselves right than in sharing ideas and feelings with the audience.

For some people, audience sensitivity comes naturally. Others have to cultivate it. If the speaker is well prepared, you can't tell the difference. Whether it's natural or acquired, the sensitivity manifests itself in subtle ways. Sensitive people don't talk down to their audiences. They don't ignore the physical needs of the people. They don't crack tasteless ethnic jokes that are likely to offend people. They don't put people down or hold them up to ridicule in front of the audience. And they speak to their audiences—large or small—as though to one person at a time.

PAY ATTENTION TO YOUR AUDIENCE

The person who is sensitive to an audience is responsive to its needs and wants. The person who is aware of the audience knows what factors are having impact on the audience at a given moment and is able to adjust the presentation accordingly.

When you're the speaker at a meeting or a conference, find out what the audience has been experiencing. Does your speech follow a significant business session at which the organization has made major decisions? Are you addressing a corporate audience that has just been told about a major reorganization? Have figures just been released showing that the company experienced a banner sales year? A disastrous sales year? Has the weather affected travel plans or interrupted recreational activities? Has there been a major local or national news event that is weighing on everyone's mind?

Your awareness of circumstances such as these will help you adjust your presentation to the mood of the audience and thus achieve maximum impact.

I remember one morning in 1978 when I was to address an audience in Indianapolis, Indiana. The night before, the world had been horrified by a stunning piece of news. The bodies of 911 followers of cult leader Jim Jones had been discovered in the jungle of the small South American nation of Guyana. They had been victims of mass suicide and executions. It happened that Jones was originally from Indianapolis.

I had planned to begin my presentation with my usual style of warm-up—a humorous introduction that got the audience to chuckling while I worked at building bridges of understanding. But I knew on this day that a light-hearted introduction would be totally inappropriate. Clearly, I had to address the issue that was on everyone's mind.

So I began by letting my audience know that I shared their sadness and concern. I expressed the hope that this event, as sorrowful as it was, might in some way contribute to a better understanding of human motives and feelings.

Eventually, I reached a point in the address when I could develop my original outline and share the humor that I had planned for the occasion. But first, I carefully laid the foundation, recognizing the trauma that the Jonestown tragedy represented for them.

UNDERSTAND YOUR AUDIENCE

Understanding your audience can mean the difference between triumph and disaster in persuading it to act. Two American presidencies illustrate the difference this understanding can make. I have already alluded to Jimmy Carter's "Malaise" speech. Carter came to the presidency in the aftermath of Watergate and Vietnam, and found a nation yearning for honest, effective leadership. As the negative consequences of the war were reinforced by the impact of the oil crisis, the president faced the nation and, in a candid and sincere address, spoke of the "malaise" that had settled on the country. He told his fellow Americans that the country faced a period of austerity.

Carter didn't understand his audience. Americans didn't want their president to tell them they were suffering from a sense of ill ease and would have to tighten their belts. They wanted a leader who would tell them that things were going to get better and that he was ready to lead them toward better times.

After a generation of taking it on the chin, Americans were ready for an upbeat message. When Ronald Reagan brought it, they listened and responded, and stayed with him, even through a deep and painful recession. Reagan understood his audience.

Different audiences will respond in different ways. You wouldn't give the same address to the Chamber of Commerce that you would give to the United Mine Workers. You wouldn't speak to a Shriners convention the way you'd speak to the American Association of University Women, or to the Jaycees the way you'd speak to the American Association of Retired People.

You gain considerable insight into an audience by getting the answers to some basic questions about the people that compose it:

♦ *What do they want out of life?*

It isn't enough to know what the people in your audience need. You also must know how they perceive their needs.

Some people are known as motivational speakers. That's a misnomer. A speaker can't motivate an audience. The audience is already motivated. It is motivated to do what it wants to do, and not what you or I want it to do.

People are like water in a faucet. The water is motivated to flow out of the faucet, but it doesn't have the opportunity until you open the tap. Many people are just as strongly motivated, and they're waiting for the opportunity to follow their motivations. The speaker who shows them that opportunity is instrumental in releasing a gush of energy.

Some people, too, are like mountain streams, which flow swiftly but follow their own channels. A good speaker shows them how to channel their motivations toward the results the speaker desires.

♦ What do they fear?

Knowledge of what people fear can be a powerful tool in channeling motivations. Sometimes you'll need to neutralize the fear. A drowning person, terrorized at the prospect of dying, will thrash and flounder, inhibiting the lifeguard's rescue efforts. But if the lifeguard can remove this fear of death, the victim will relax and cooperate with the rescuer.

On the other hand, a person who is inclined to get behind the wheel after imbibing too many martinis needs a healthy dose of fear—the fear of tragic death, either to the driver or to others in the path of the driver.

The more you know about your audience's fears, the better you will be able to establish effective communication.

♦ What do they know?

If somebody from out of town calls and asks directions to your place, the first thing you normally ask is "Where are you now?"

You have to know where people are before you can tell them how to reach their destinations.

The process is similar in any kind of communication. There has to be a point of origin and there has to be a destination.

The point of origin is what the audience already knows, understands or believes. The destination is what you want the audience to know, understand or believe after you've finished talking.

So when you speak to an audience, you must start on common

266

ground. You must know what the audience knows or believes. Otherwise, you won't know where to begin the presentation.

After you've established that common ground, you have to retain it throughout the presentation.

Some people, when they're speaking on their area of expertise, like to impress their audience with how much they know. That's a sure way to lose an audience. Your purpose is not to impress people with your knowledge, but to communicate your knowledge in such a way that they will be influenced to do the things you want them to do.

Speakers shouldn't worry about whether they know more than the audience or the audience knows more than they. If you think you know more than your audience knows, you may come across as condescending. If you think your audience knows more than you do, you may feel a bit intimidated.

It's best to think of yourself as neither inferior nor superior to your audience; just different. You know things your audience doesn't know, and the individuals in the audience know things you don't know. Neither is inferior or superior to the other.

♦ *What do they understand?*

There's a big difference between knowing and understanding. When you're driving, it's not enough to know that the light over the intersection is red. You must also understand that a red light means you must stop.

The American audience that saw Nikita Khrushchev hold his clenched hands above his head knew what the Soviet leader was doing. But the audience didn't understand that it was a gesture of friendliness and not an act of braggadocio. Other incidents of international misunderstanding are more humorous.

Let me relate one other example of the difference between knowing and understanding.

A small community in a poultry-growing region was holding a festival to celebrate the industry that was the backbone of its economy. As part of the festivity, 4-H youngsters entered a poultry contest. The chickens they had raised were on display, all plucked and cleaned and ready for the cooking pot. Representatives of the area's supermarkets were there, vying for the honor of offering their customers the prize-winning product while reaping some favorable publicity.

An out-of-town visitor arrived late just as the bidding was reaching its climax.

"I'm offered nine dollars; who'll make it ten?" chanted the auctioneer.

The visitor looked at the boxes of high-quality poultry—about 30 pounds of it. Ten dollars seemed like a steal.

"Ten dollars," he called, and the auctioneer said "Sold."

The visitor came forward, taking a crisp $10 from his wallet.

"That'll be $300," said the auctioneer.

The visitor was mortified. He *knew* he had bid $10 for the poultry. He *understood* that he was bidding $10 for the whole batch. Had he arrived at the start of the auction, he would have known that he was bidding $10 *per pound.*

So when you're speaking to an audience, be alert for any misunderstanding and be prepared to deal with it promptly. When you're asking $10, make sure your audience understands that you mean "per pound."

IDENTIFY WITH YOUR AUDIENCE

If you want to captivate your audience, you must be able to see through the eyes and hear through the ears of your listeners. That means identifying with the audience. When members of your audience perceive you as one of them instead of as an outsider, you've arrived as a communicator.

If you can use the word "we" to embrace yourself and the audience—and your listeners accept the embrace—then you have their attention.

The framers of the Constitution of the United States faced a huge communications task. The people of the former colonies thought of themselves as New Englanders, New Yorkers, Virginians, or Carolinians first, and as Americans second. In the public consciousness, "United States" was a plural descriptive and not the name of a nation. How were the founders of the republic to promote the idea that the settlers from Maine to Georgia were a single people and not 13 different nationalities?

The preamble to the Constitution helped set the tone. It read:

> *We the people of the United States, in order to form a more perfect union, establish justice, insure domestic tranquility, provide for the common defense, promote the general welfare, and secure the blessings of liberty to ourselves and our posterity do ordain and establish this Constitution for the United States of America.*

The phrase "We the people" (as opposed to "We the peoples) helped establish the oneness of Americans, though it took a civil war to establish once and for all that this was "one nation, indivisible." The framers didn't present the Constitution as a gift from them to the people, but as a creation of the people themselves. Instead of guaranteeing freedom for "you and your posterity," they undertook to "secure the blessings of liberty for **ourselves** and **our** posterity" (emphasis mine).

As a speaker, look for ways to achieve oneness with your audience. The more you identify with the circumstances, needs and feelings of your audience, the easier it is for your audience to identify with you.

On the way to achieving this oneness, however, you will encounter many barriers. Some of them can be avoided and others can be overcome. The next chapter shows you how to deal with them.

CHAPTER

21

Conquering the Barriers

Every speaker hopes for the perfect occasion. The layout of the room is perfect; every seat in the house is the best seat in the house. The audience is alert, receptive and friendly. The sound system works splendidly and the acoustics are ideal. There are no visual or auditory distractions while you speak. Your voice is great, your timing is perfect, your audiovisual materials are in the right order and right side up, and the equipment works. Your introduction is an attention-grabber, the audience stays involved throughout the presentation, and your smashing conclusion brings the whole room to its feet.

When you encounter all these conditions, mark the date on your calendar. Break out the champagne and celebrate it year after year. You're not likely to encounter such an experience again in your lifetime. In public speaking, as in most other endeavors, Murphy's Law is alive and well: If anything can go wrong, it will. (O'Toole's Law says that Murphy was an optimist.)

That doesn't faze accomplished speakers. They know that unexpected glitches will occur, and they're prepared to deal with them.

AVOID IMPENETRABLE BARRIERS

Many barriers can be anticipated and sometimes removed in advance. Some barriers are impenetrable, however. A good football coach knows that when it's fourth down and nine yards to go on your own 20-yard-line, you don't run the ball unless you're in desperate straits. The best strategy is to fall back and punt.

Good speakers, too, know when to punt. Dr. Martin Luther King Jr. was a courageous man, but he didn't waste his breath preaching racial harmony to Ku Klux Klan audiences.

NEVER SPEAK FOLLOWING A LONG COCKTAIL HOUR

I once spoke at a banquet in a beautiful resort hotel in Hilton Head, South Carolina. When I arrived, I noticed a cocktail party in progress. It had started at 3 P.M., and the waiters were still taking orders for drinks when I was introduced. The audience was drunk, and was even throwing bread rolls from one table to another. There was no way I could inform, persuade or inspire this audience. The experience taught me never to accept an engagement in which I'm scheduled to speak immediately after a long cocktail party.

TRYING TO BEAT THE BAND

Congressman Jim Wright of Texas, who was then speaker of the U. S. House of Representatives, encountered another impossible situation when he addressed the annual meeting of the National Conference of Editorial Writers in Fort Worth, Texas. Immediately behind the platform from which he spoke was a partition that divided the large meeting hall into two rooms.

The speaker made a few preliminary remarks, then opened the floor for questions. Just as the meatier questions were coming in, the room exploded with noise. On the other side of that partition was a rock band, which was providing music for a dance. The band had agreed to keep silent until 9 P.M. The editorial writers' program went a few minutes past 9, and the band refused to wait any longer.

The noise was so loud that people sitting at the tables couldn't hear each other, much less the speaker. The meeting planners tried to persuade the band to hold off for a few more minutes, but the band refused. Wright did the only thing he could do under the circumstances: He threw up his hands and sat down.

COMPETITION AND RESISTANCE

The barriers to communicating from the platform fall roughly into two categories: competition and resistance.

The crusader who tries to sell gun control to a group of National Rifle Association members is encountering resistance. This takes the form of an emotional or intellectual reluctance to hear what is being said. Jim Wright was encountering competition: The noise from the band successfully competed against his voice for the ears of his audience.

The best way to confront these barriers is to avoid them. Don't accept an invitation to address an audience that you know you have no chance of reaching or persuading. And work with the program chairman in advance to head off any possible competition for your presentation.

FACTORS TO MONITOR

Here are some environmental factors to monitor in advance:

♦ *Physical layout*

The size and shape of a room can be a critical factor in the success of your speech. I once spoke to a group in the expansive ballroom of the Dunes Hotel in Las Vegas. The room could have accommodated a group four times as large as the one I addressed. The audience did what audiences normally do: The people moved to the rear of the auditorium. This created a distance between me and those who came to hear me.

When this sort of situation arises, you have to remember the proverb: If the mountain won't come to Mohammed, then Mohammed must go to the mountain. In this case, the ballroom was equipped with spotlights and long microphone cords. I was able to move to the audience and to interact with it.

A room that is too small can be at least as bad. When people are crowded into a small space, they feel packed in and it's hard for them to give you their full attention.

Acoustics have a major effect on the way your message is perceived. In some rooms, if you turn down the sound system, the audience can't hear you. If you turn it up, it sounds like you're in a cave. If you have anything to say about the choice of settings, choose a room appropriate for the size of the group, with acoustics appropriate for your presentation. If you have to speak under unfavorable circumstances, plan for them in advance, as I did in the case of the Dunes engagement.

♦ *Temperature and lighting*

When people get warm and the lights are dim, they tend to get drowsy—especially if they've just been wined and dined. When the room is too cool, people get fidgety, their minds focused more on their discomfort than on anything you might have to say. When the lights are too bright, they can destroy any feeling of intimacy between speaker and audience. Bright lights, too, can cause people to become edgy and tense.

The best time to check out these conditions is before you stand up to speak. When you're ready to speak, your mind should be free to concentrate on your message and your audience. Remember that when you stand up to speak, your excitement will probably make you warmer than most people in your audience. Monitor your audience as you speak. If you sense that the people are physically uncomfortable, stop and try to do something about it. Isn't that what all good hosts would do for their guests?

♦ *Faulty equipment*

It's amazing how many conference centers will spend millions on an auditorium, then balk at spending a few hundred dollars for a decent public-address system.

In most cases, you're at the mercy of the public-address system when it comes to conveying your words to the audience. So arrive early and check it out. Take care of any problems before you mount the platform. Talk to the people who will be operating the equipment. Make sure they understand your needs and wishes.

If you're using audio-visual aids, make sure the equipment is functioning before you get up to speak. If you're going to be operating it, be sure you know how it works.

♦ *Visual distractions*

Maybe you think what you have to say is more interesting than anything that could possibly be going on around you. But don't tell that to an audience within clear view of a swimming pool populated with shapely mermaids in brief attire or muscular Adonises with pectorals on display. You're quite likely to lose out.

So if you have any influence over the setting, get a room with no competing views to contend with.

You may have to deal with other types of distractions. It's hard for a speaker to maintain rapport with an audience while waiters are bringing in the flaming dessert or are removing dishes from the table. It's hard to compete with bright photographic flashes or with television klieg lights.

If possible, arrange for these distractions to take place at a time when you're not speaking. If any of them interrupt your speech, it's usually best to stop until the distraction has passed.

♦ *Noises.*

When you're speaking, your voice should be the loudest sound in the room by far. If other noises compete, you're struggling to retain the audience's attention. I've competed with jackhammers breaking up concrete, with kitchen workers playing or fighting, with low-flying aircraft, and with other meetings or parties nearby.

Sometimes you have to compete with pleasant sounds—soft, piped-in music or a band performing in the next room.

It's best to find out about your competition in advance, do what you can to eliminate it, and if that's impossible, develop a strategy for dealing with it.

MONITOR THE AUDIENCE

When you're addressing an audience, keep a close watch on everything your listeners do. Be alert for signs that you're losing their attention or that they're having trouble following you. Are the people on the back rows straining to hear you? Can everyone see you clearly, and can they see any visual aids you might be using?

If the people in your audience start out alert and attentive but later start fidgeting and slumping in their chairs, it usually means that the environment is uncomfortable for some reason. Find out why, and take care of the problem before you proceed.

If you know your listeners have been sitting in one position for a long time, perhaps in uncomfortable chairs, give them a break. Involve them in a stand-up exercise or call a short recess to give people a chance to visit the rest rooms.

OVERCOMING AUDIENCE RESISTANCE

Barriers resulting from audience resistance can be just as formidable as those resulting from environmental conditions.

I once spoke at a major meeting of the Diamond Shamrock Corporation in Florida. I didn't know until I arrived that my audience would include people from all over the world. Many of them knew little English. A fast-paced speech full of witty colloquialisms would have forfeited the attention of a significant proportion of this audience. So I developed a strategy. I spoke slowly and distinctly. And I wove into my speech some stories about my own experiences in learning the language and customs of the American people. The strategy enabled me to gain and hold the attention of the foreign visitors and further enhance the international flair of the meeting.

On another occasion, I was asked to give an inspirational speech to the sales force of a large air-brakes manufacturer in Saginaw, Michigan. What I didn't know when I accepted the invitation was that just before I spoke the company was to announce a major shake-up in the sales division. I therefore found myself speaking to many people who had seen their territories restructured and some who had seen their incomes reduced.

Since I was there at the invitation of management, it was natural for the audience to assume that I was somehow involved in all the changes, or at least knew about them.

Under such circumstances, you don't pretend you don't know what has happened and you don't stand up and crack jokes about other people's misfortunes. You let the audience know that you care. And you look for positives in the situation.

DIAGNOSE AUDIENCE RESPONSE

If you look and listen carefully, audience response will tell you whether you are encountering emotional or intellectual resistance. Audience response is to the public speaker what symptoms are to a doctor. Sensitive speakers know what audience response to expect, and when they don't get it, they look for the reasons.

One technique for testing the degree to which you're getting through to the audience is to ask a question periodically that can be answered with one word. If the audience shouts back the answer, you know you've connected. If only a few respond, you need to find out why you're losing your audience.

BECOME PHYSICALLY INVOLVED WITH THE AUDIENCE

It's an unusual day when I don't get up and speak to some group. Over the years, I've learned a few secrets for breaking down the barriers to communication between speaker and audience.

One of the most effective is to become physically involved with the audience. You may feel safer hiding behind the dais or standing with several rows of empty seats between you and the audience. But you can't carry on dialogue with an audience that is isolated from you.

POOR ME VS. THE GREAT GIPPER

One of the toughest pieces of competition I had came at a meeting of the Associated General Contractors of America. I was scheduled to speak in the afternoon. The mid-morning speaker was a man named Ronald Reagan, who at the time was living at 1600 Pennsylvania Avenue in Washington, D.C.

There are worse fates than following Ronald Reagan on the platform. I discovered one of them very quickly. For some reason, the president had to reschedule his speech for the exact time that I was to speak. So guess who most people went to hear? Hey, I've overcome some tough obstacles, but I can't match the president's clout. Instead of an audience of several hundred, I faced an audience of about 30.

But what an audience! These people had to be committed if they were willing to pass up a speech by the Gipper in favor of one by Nido Qubein. So I tried twice as hard to please them. I called them to the front of the room, and we sat around in a circle. The speech turned into a group discussion. The audience became so involved that it was hard to break it up at the appointed time.

GET THE AUDIENCE PHYSICALLY INVOLVED WITH YOU

Another technique is to get your audience physically involved with you. You can do this with any number of simple devices that don't require intense mental effort or manual dexterity. One of my favorites is the hand-clapping game.

I used·it to good effect once when I shared the platform with Dave Thomas, founder of Wendy's, and Bill Leonard, then president of CBS News. The occasion was the Western Kentucky University Free Enterprise Fair, and the audience was made up of several thousand high-school and college students who were there for a good time.

I had spoken six times that week to major corporate and association groups. This definitely called for a change of pace.

So I asked the students to clap their hands when I crossed my hands, but not to clap when my hands weren't crossed. At first they acted on signal. But when I began faking the crossing of my hands and speeding up the tempo, they soon became confused. I kept working at it until everyone in the audience was involved.

This may not work as well with the stockholders of IBM, but with the appropriate group it's a good warm-up exercise that can grab the attention of those in your audience and prepare them to listen to you.

Older audiences can be captivated by equally simple devices. Once, speaking at the River Oaks Country Club in Houston, I asked how many of the men present dominated their wives. Only one held up his hand. That brought a laugh. But when his wife stood up and pushed his arm down, she brought down the house.

Obviously, a routine can be staged if you set it up with the right person. Involving an individual from the audience can be an effective way of catching the attention of everyone—especially when the individual involved is well-known and well-liked. But remember the words of caution I passed on earlier: Make sure the individual involved has a good sense of humor and is a willing participant. And avoid embarrassing or putting down the individual. The people in the audience identify with the individual chosen from their ranks more than they do with you. Send the person back into the audience with a word of commendation on being such a good sport, and ask the audience to applaud the good sport. This will make your confederate from the audience feel good and will identify you with the audience.

When you use an exercise to involve the audience, follow these guidelines:

- Keep it simple.
- Make it move.
- Make it short.
- Make it fun for everybody.
- Make it fit your audience and situation.

A DUAL MEDIUM: SIGHT AND SOUND

A platform speech is a dual medium. It communicates through the ears and it communicates through the eyes. So when you're addressing an audience, look alive. Be relaxed but enthusiastic. Let your face, your hands and your posture communicate mood and meaning to your audience.

The audience will read meaning into your body language whether you are conscious or unconscious of what you're doing. If your hands hang limply by your side, the audience infers that you're scared. Hands folded across the chest tell your listeners that you're defensive. Hands nervously fidgeting with your glasses or notes tell everyone that you're self-conscious. Use your hands for natural, purposeful gestures, the way you do when you're holding an enthusiastic conversation with an individual.

And let your face and voice come alive. A monotone drones people to sleep. A blank expression says "Nothing I'm saying is worth getting excited about."

Speak in your lower voice range to convey a feeling of confidence, but modulate your voice to show various degrees of excitement, concern, anger or conviction. And let your face reveal your emotions. Don't try to fake it; just let your feelings show.

When you're in front of an audience, let yourself unwind. You have an appealing personality. Let it come through. Use every natural charm at your disposal to captivate the audience.

Let your style fit your audience. I used the hand-clapping routine with the high-school students from Kentucky, not with the contractors who chose to hear me instead of President Reagan.

Good communicators are so attuned to their audiences that they can make every individual think, "These words are meant just for me."

USE VISUAL AIDS

The audiences of the 21st century have grown up with television, movies, and videotapes. They're even adding the sight dimension to their phone conversations. They are more visually oriented than any previous generation. When they come to hear you talk, they bring their eyes as well as their ears. If they were there only to listen, they could get it all from an audiotape.

So visual aids can be the battering rams with which you break down walls of resistance to your message. They can help you get the audience completely involved with your presentation.

One method I sometimes use is to display several common items—perhaps a key, a paper clip, a cup or a pencil, on an opaque projector. After I've given members of the audience a minute to observe them, I turn off the projector and ask them to write down a list of all the things displayed. This leads into a discussion of how little we tend to observe the common things around us and how hard it is to remember even a few things.

When you use visual aids, keep these suggestions in mind:

♦ Keep them simple—never more than three lines on a slide.
♦ Convey only one message per visual.
♦ Make sure the visual calls attention to you and your message and doesn't distract your audience.
♦ Practice using the visuals until you can do it naturally and comfortably.
♦ Before you begin the presentation, make sure the audiovisual tools are all in working condition.
♦ Keep your visual aids short.
♦ Apply them to what you're saying.
♦ Test the audience's response to them.

OVERCOMING STAGE FRIGHT

For many people, the greatest barrier to communication from the public platform is in their own minds. About 40% of Americans suffer from "performance anxiety," also known as stage fright. It's believed to be the most widespread phobia in the United States.

Stage fright can be overcome. Part of the remedy is a change in your attitude toward the speech.

According to Michael T. Motley, Ph.D., stage fright is most common among people who look upon a speech as a performance rather than an exercise in communication. They go to the platform convinced that the room is full of critics who will be evaluating their gestures, language and posture. This anxiety leads them to assume the role of actors, adopting formal, artificial language and behavior that they assume to be better than their normal, natural ways of expressing themselves.[1]

You can overcome this tendency by looking upon your speech as an opportunity to communicate your thoughts and ideas to the audience. Concentrate on the message, not on the performance. Think of the main ideas you want to communicate, and think of how you want to put them across.

Practice your speech before one or two individuals. Talk as if you're conversing with those individuals. Use your notes to remind you of what you want to say. You'll probably feel silly delivering an oration to just one or two people, so don't orate. Talk to them conversationally, using the language, inflections and gestures you use in ordinary conversation.

When you get on the platform, follow the same technique. Look at specific individuals in the audience and speak to them one person at a time. When you're talking to individuals, you keep your language natural and you overcome the feeling that you're giving a performance.

Motley provides these additional tips:

♦ Put yourself in your audience's place. Be aware that your audience consists of individuals with differing interests and attitudes and different degrees of familiarity with your topic. Speak to them in their terms and in their language.

♦ Don't memorize and don't read. Use the extemporaneous approach.

♦ Forget about your hands and facial expressions. Concentrate on the message you want to convey and let your nonverbal communication take its natural course.

♦ Adopt a calm, unhurried pace. You're there to impart understanding, not to "get it over with." [2]

Burton J. Rubin, author of *The Stage Fright Handbook,* notes that many speakers get into trouble by thinking ahead to what *might* happen. Their fears of "going blank" or committing some verbal blunder become self-fulfilling prophecies.

The remedy is to "stay in the present." One way of doing this is to select some object in the room—a table, chair, sofa or lectern—

and concentrate on it. This will keep your mind from becoming crowded with "what ifs."

Another technique is to concentrate on the words you want to stress and the way you're going to interpret your material. If you're thinking about these things, you won't have the mental capacity to think ahead and worry about the "what ifs."

If you should go blank, don't panic. It happens to everybody. The ideas and words you want are in your brain; you just need to take a moment to find them. So pause for a moment. A little silence never hurt anyone. Forget the audience, forget your anxiety and just concentrate on remembering. Retrace your train of thoughts, one thought at a time. It'll come.[3]

NERVOUS OR NOT, BE YOURSELF

The advice to "be yourself" applies regardless of whether you suffer from stage fright.

Adopt a style that accords with your personality. If you're normally a quiet, dignified individual, don't hop, skip and jump to the platform as if you can't wait to fire up your audience. The best way to approach the podium is with calm, confident stride. Face your audience and smile. Then begin your speech.

Establish good eye contact at the outset. Effective speakers don't speak to the crowd. They speak to the individuals in the crowd. Don't look at the back of the room and don't let your gaze wonder vaguely over the audience. Look individuals in the eyes. Look for people who return your look with friendly, interested expressions. Maintain eye contact long enough to achieve mutual understanding, then move on to the next person.

Public speaking can be one of the most rewarding forms of communication. When you find yourself firing up an audience, the energy flows both ways. Master the medium. The skills you develop in addressing a live audience will serve you well in the 21st century.

EPILOGUE

———

Throughout this book, we've demonstrated that words are more than sounds entering the ear; more than ink patterns on paper.

They convey meaning. They convey instruction, information, and inspiration. They convey power. And in business, they have a strong effect on the bottom line.

What Benjamin Disraeli, the 19th-century British statesman, observed still applies: "All other things being equal, the person who succeeds will be the person with the best information." And information can be acquired only through communication.

So, as you can see, the ability to communicate with precision has a tremendous impact on corporate profits.

EDUCATE, DON'T TRAIN

In other times, management could rely on repetitive training to equip the work force to carry out its tasks. But, as Stanley Marcus once said, "You don't train people; you train dogs and elephants; you educate people."

Today's work force needs more than training in how to turn screws and how to pull levers. It must be educated to communicate properly. An organization's success depends heavily on the ability to achieve alignment among all the people who work for it. That alignment cannot be achieved without effective communication to unify the people toward a common vision, a common mission and common goals.

An organization is also dependent for its success on the ability to innovate and to change. Innovation and change flow from powerful ideas that germinate within the work force and are communicated across functional boundaries and up and down through management levels.

We've spent entirely too much time in the past teaching people what to do instead of concentrating on how they think and how they feel and how they behave; far too much time getting a job done instead of producing excellent results; far too much time conforming instead of creating.

Successful corporations need work forces made up of people educated in such skills as goal-setting, problem-solving and decision-making, conflict management, and other communication skills.

PENETRATING THE BARRIER

According to philosopher William James, "The most immutable barrier in nature is between one man's thoughts and another's."

Penetrating that barrier is the greatest challenge of 21st century communication.

Peter Drucker claims that more than 60% of all management problems result from breakdowns in communication.

Efficiency experts claim that at least 40% of the average worker's time is spent doing tasks that are either unnecessary or have to be done over because they were not done according to instructions.

Executives can multiply their influence by learning the techniques of persuasive communication. High-powered communicators learn to focus words the way a laser beam focuses light.

AT THE HEART OF EVERYTHING

Communication is at the heart of everything we do. It is the foundation for interaction among human beings. Communication has to do with meanings, with understandings, with feelings, with desires, with needs and with ideas.

Our world is filled with information, but that isn't enough. We need understanding, and that calls for transcending that "immutable barrier" between one person's thoughts and another's; for bridging the distance between human beings so that we can better live together, work together, get along with each other and make this earth the best possible home for the human race.

It is my hope that this book will help you build bridges to your staff, your employees, to your customers, and to everyone who plays a meaningful role in your career and your life.

End Notes

Chapter One

1. Lennie Copeland, "Four by Four: How Do You Manage a Diverse Work Force?" *Training & Development Journal,* February 1989, p. 18.

2. James M. Kouzes and Barry Z. Posner, "The Credibility Factor: What Followers Expect From Their Leaders," *Management Review,* January 1990, p. 29.

Chapter Two

1. *Ernest Hemingway, Dateline: Toronto,* (New York: Charles Scribner's Sons, 1985).

Chapter Four

1. Floyd Wickman, *The Wickman Formula: Seven Steps to Achieving Your Full Potential* (High Point, N.C.: Executive Press, 1991) p. 96.

2. Ed Temple with B'Lou Carter, Only the Pure in Heart Survive, (Nashville TN: Broadman Press, 1980) p. 94.

Chapter Six

1. Katharine LeMee, Language Today: A Survey of Current Linguistic Thought (New York: Funk & Wagnalls, 1967), Mario Pei, editor and chief

contributor, with William F. Marquardt, Katherine LeMee and Don L. F. Nilsen. pp. 102–105.

2. Ibid.

Chapter Seven

1. Robert Howard, "Values Make the Company: An Interview with Robert Haas," *Harvard Business Review,* September/October 1990, pp. 134–142.

Chapter Eight

1. Michael Rothschild, "Want to Grow? Watch Your Language," Forbes ASAP, October 25, 1993, p. 20.

Chapter Nine

1. "Face-to-Face: Managing the Journey," *INC.,* November 1990, p. 46.

Chapter Ten

1. Casey Miller and Kate Swift, *Words and Women, New Language in New Times* (Garden City, N.Y.: Anchor Press/Doubleday. 1976), p. 108.

2. Ibid, pp. 109–110.

3. Ibid, pp. 109–110.

4. Deborah Tannen, Ph.D., *You Just Don't Understand* (New York: William Morrow and Company, Inc., 1990) pp. 24–25.

5. Barbara Gamarekian (New York Times News Service), "Book looks at poor communication between the sexes," *The News and Observer,* Raleigh, N.C., June 30, 1991, p. 10E.

6. Ibid., pp. 109–110.

7. Molly Ivins, *Atlanta Journal-Constitution,* August 29, 1993, p. D5.

Chapter Eleven

1. "Four by Four," *Training and Development Journal,* February 1989.

2. Katherine LeMee, *Language Today: A Survey of Current Linguis-*

tic Thought, (New York: Funk & Wagnalls, 1967), Mario Pei, editor and chief contributor, p. 123.

Chapter Twelve

1. David Russell, director of custom communications for GTE Telephone Operations in Dallas, as quoted in *Nation's Business,* May 1993, Page 28.

Chapter Nineteen

1. Dyan Machan, "How You Can Get a Few Good Laughs," *Reader's Digest,* December 1991, pp. 79–80, as reprinted from *Forbes,* October 15, 1990.

Chapter Twenty-One

1. Michael T. Motley, "Taking the Terror Out of Talk," *Psychology Today,* January 1988, p. 47.

2. Ibid. p. 49.

3. Burton J. Rubin, *Stage Fright Handbook* (Saratoga Springs, N.Y.: Decision-Making Systems Ltd, 1986) p. 2.

About the Author

———

Nido Qubein is president of High Point University and chairman of Great Harvest Bread Co. (220 stores in 43 states).

He serves on the boards of several national organizations including BB&T Corporation (with $190 billion in assets), the La-Z-Boy Corporation (one of the largest and most recognized furniture brands worldwide), the National Speakers Association Foundation (which he founded in 1983), and the Qubein Foundation (which has awarded more than 600 Scholarships to deserving college students).

He has been the recipient of many honors, including the Horatio Alger Award for Distinguished Americans, the Order of the Long Leaf Pine (North Carolina's highest civic award), several honorary doctorates, the Ellis Island Medal of Honor, The Cavett (known as the Oscar of the speaking profession), Toastmasters International Golden Gavel, the Sales and Marketing International Hall of Fame, Alexis de'Tocqueville Award, Citizen of the Year and Philanthropist of the Year in High Point, North Carolina, where he resides.

Dr. Qubein is in great demand as a speaker at conventions, sales meetings, and executive conferences internationally. His books and audio/visual learning programs are translated in a dozen languages. You may reach him at: nqubein@highpoint.edu.

For Further Information

———

For information about High Point University,
please call or write:

High Point University
833 Montlieu Avenue
High Point, NC 27262 USA
Telephone (336) 841-9000
Facsimile (336) 841-4599

www.highpoint.edu

For information on Nido Qubein's
speeches and consulting call or write:

Consulting Resources, Inc.
806 Westchester Drive
High Point, NC 27262 USA
Telephone (336) 889-3010
Facsimile (336) 885-1829

For a photo gallery, learning resources, downloads, and
dozens of free articles and self-evaluation quizzes, visit:

www.nidoqubein.com

NOTES

NOTES

NOTES

NOTES

NOTES

NOTES

NOTES